Unmasking Japan Today

UNMASKING JAPAN TODAY

The Impact of
Traditional Values on
Modern Japanese Society

FUMIE KUMAGAI
with the assistance of
Donna J. Keyser

PRAEGER

Westport, Connecticut
London

Library of Congress Cataloging-in-Publication Data

Kumagai, Fumie.
    Unmasking Japan today : the impact of traditional values on modern
Japanese society / by Fumie Kumagai with the assistance of Donna J.
Keyser.
        p.   cm.
    Includes bibliographical references and index.
    ISBN 0–275–95144–8 (alk. paper)
    1. Japan—Social conditions—1945– . 2. Japan—Social life and
customs—20th century.   3. Social values—Japan—History—20th
century.   I. Keyser, Donna J.   II. Title.
HN723.5.K756   1996
306'.0952—dc20   95–23224

British Library Cataloguing in Publication Data is available.

Library of Congress Catalog Card Number: 95–23224
ISBN: 0–275–95144–8

First published in 1996

Praeger Publishers, 88 Post Road West, Westport, CT 06881
An imprint of Greenwood Publishing Group, Inc.

Printed in the United States of America

The paper used in this book complies with the
Permanent Paper Standard issued by the National
Information Standards Organization (Z39.48–1984).

10 9 8 7 6 5 4 3 2 1

Contents

Figures   vii

Preface   ix

Introduction: The Process of Japanese Modernization   1

Part I. The Japanese Family—Change and Continuity

1.   Changes in the Japanese Family System   15

2.   Popular Culture/Lifestyles of the Japanese Family   31

3.   Emerging Family Problems   47

Part II. Education and Youth

4.   The Japanese Educational System   61

5.   Japanese Youth Today   73

Part III.   Women and Labor Force Participation

6.   The Changing Status of Women   93

7.   Japanese Women in the Workforce   107

Part IV.   The Graying of Japan

8.   Aging as a Sociocultural Process   123

9.   The Economics of Aging   139

10.   The Impact of Aging on Family Relations   147

Conclusion: From Modernization to Internationalization 157

References   161

Index   187

Figures

I–1.   A Dual Structural Model of Japanese Society   5

I–2.   Changes in Labor Force Participation Rate by
       Industry: 1920–1992   6

I–3.   Changes in the Farm Household Proportion by the
       Type of Participation: 1941–1990   7

1–1.   The Modified Stem Family in Japan   26

2–1.   Changes in the Rate of the Middle-Class
       Identification: 1958–1993   35

4–1.   Japanese School System   63

4–2.   Changes in the Number of Foreign Students
       Studying at Japanese Higher Educational Institutions
       by Type of Funds: 1978–1993   71

5–1.   Importance of the Goals in the Life of Junior High
       School Students in Japan and the United States:
       Proportions of Very Important   77

5–2.   The Degree of Agreement in Lifestyles among High

School Students in Japan, the United States, and Taiwan   81

5–3.   Changes in the Number of Schools and Teachers Having School Violence Problems: 1982–1992   84

6–1.   Changes in Attitudes toward ''Men's Place Is at Work and Women's Place Is at Home'': 1979–1992   101

7–1.   Changes in Labor Force Participation Rates: 1920–1992   108

7–2.   Changes in Labor Force Participation Rates of Japanese Women by Age: 1960, 1970, 1980, and 1990   110

8–1.   Changes in the Proportion of the Elderly Sixty-Five and Over in Five Countries: 1900–2025   125

8–2.   Changes in Percent Distributions of the Japanese Population by Three Age Groups: 1884–2020   126

8–3.   Changes and Projections of Life Expectancy at Birth of Japanese Male and Female: 1920–2025   128

8–4.   Changes in the Proportion of the Japanese Elderly by Age Group: 1930–2025   130

8–5.   The Proportion of Care Providers by Whom One Desires to Be Taken Care of When Becoming Old and Frail by Sex and Age Group   133

9–1.   Changes in the Growth of the Silver Market by Industry: 1980–2000   144

10–1.   Changes in Living Arrangements of the Elderly Sixty-Five and Over: 1960–1990   148

Preface

It was more than ten years ago when I first started to discover that Japan was not nearly as modern as it presented itself. Having lived in the United States for nearly fifteen years by that time, I had come to the point where I could view my own country with the objectivity gained from valuable comparative insight. I realized then that a true understanding of Japan required a dual structural perspective, one that reveals the integrated coexistence of both modernity and tradition in contemporary Japanese society. This book is the product of that realization.

"Coming out of the long tunnel I saw snow country," writes Japanese author Yasunari Kawabata when he begins his tale of *Yukiguni* (The Snow Country) (1937, 1). The snow-covered land at the tunnel's end forms a nearly perfect juxtaposition to the sunny winter day the narrator has left behind in Tokyo—and this in just one brief ride through the Shimizu Tunnel, which connects the Pacific Ocean and Japan Sea sides of our small island country. The contrast that Kawabata describes is one that permeates the very fabric of Japanese society, and his vision has inspired me to write of Japan as it truly is: a rich and unique blend of tradition and modernity.

Twenty years ago as a student of sociology, I was fortunate to be advised by Professors William H. Sewell of the University of Wisconsin and Murray A. Straus of the University of New Hampshire. It was through their wisdom and guidance that I came to see the contribution I might make as a Japan specialist willing to analyze my own country from an "outsider's" perspective.

In those years, of course, study of Japan among Americans and other non-Japanese was fairly limited; few could imagine that Japan would emerge as a major economic power and thus become a source of world-wide interest. Even general knowledge of Japan was severely lacking. As unbelievable as it now seems, people often asked me: "Is Japan a jungle?" "Do you know SONY?" or "Do people in Japan still practice *hara kiri*?" In many ways, Japan was invisible to the international community at that time.

Much has changed in the intervening years. News of Japan floods radio and TV networks around the world, articles and books on Japan and its people are forever being published, and even movies featuring Japan are current box office hits. Nevertheless, the level of understanding of Japan among the average American population remains somewhat distorted. This is due in part to the reluctance of Japanese to reveal their true identity and also in part to the lack of realization among Japanese themselves that tradition still plays an important role in modern Japanese society. My hope is that *Unmasking Japan Today* will help to narrow this gap in understanding between Japanese and Americans, as well as others in Japan and throughout the world.

Bringing this project to successful completion has required a lot of work and a lot of time. Fortunately, I was able to convince my friend and colleague Dr. Donna J. Keyser to assist me in rewriting, editing, and bringing the manuscript to publishable form. Dr. Keyser has spent a number of years living and studying in Japan and, perhaps because of this, always seemed to know intuitively what I was trying to say and how I should best say it.

Sincere acknowledgment is also extended to various individuals and institutions, for without their cooperation and warm support, this project could not have been accomplished. The office of the Honorable Congressman Kazuo Aichi has graciously assisted my procurement of government publications and survey data, making it possible for me to incorporate up-to-date statistics on Japan in this manuscript. Professor Koya Azumi, an American-trained sociologist of organization, provided invaluable guidance in directing me to study Japan; Professor Kiyomi Morioka, an eminent family sociologist, was most generous in his insightful and provocative criticisms on the topic; and Professor Takao

Suzuki, a world-reknowned sociolinguist, inspired me with his keen intuition and unique perspective on the analysis of Japanese society.

Finally, special appreciation is extended to Kyorin University for its generosity in providing financial support through the Graduate School Research Project Grants for my work on this project and partial support for the publication of this book. Without this support, I would not have been able to complete the numerous tasks required to publish this book.

Introduction: The Process of Japanese Modernization

Japan's recent emergence as a major economic power has created a worldwide surge of interest in the nation and its people. Even in the face of a severe and prolonged recession, Japan today is economically powerful, culturally rich, and politically free and stable (i.e., there has been no domestic war in its recent history), ranking in all these respects among the leading nations of the world. But how modern is modern-day Japan? In actuality, Japan is not nearly as modern as it presents itself; the essence of Japanese society is an integration of both modernity and tradition. Like the two-headed Janus, Japan can show one face at one time and a completely different face at another.

Some of the difficulty that people have understanding Japanese society today stems from the complex nature of Japan's modernization. Three major cultures have left an imprint on Japan: Oriental, European, and American. Nevertheless, it is striking to note that throughout this process Japan never lost its own identity and cultural specificity. In each phase of its modernization, there emerged a blending of cultures where the ideas and manners borrowed from outside cultures retained unique Japanese characteristics.

Part of this is no doubt due to Japan's geographical insularity: It is an island nation having little or no historical or cultural affinity with its

Southeast Asian neighbors, despite some linguistic similarities that may exist. While the Japanese government sent missions abroad to study the essence of other countries' technological, scientific, and cultural civilization, only a very limited number of foreigners came to Japan to be directly involved in the modernization process. Never having been colonized by another foreign power, Japan's cultural assimilation lacked any sustained human contact with the outside world. As a result of this cultural self-colonization,[1] the nation's racial and ethnic homogeneity has remained intact, permitting Japanese to modernize society while still preserving a sense of their own special identity.[2]

ORIENTALIZATION

During the first phase of Japanese modernization from the sixth to eighth centuries, Chinese thought and practices permeated Japanese society. *Wakon kansai* (i.e., Chinese learning and Japanese spirit) is the ground upon which modern-day Japan exists. It is a unique blend of diametrically opposed modes of religious perception: an intuitive, non-reflective "mythic" mode represented by Japan's indigenous Shinto religion, a strong sense of ancestor worship stemming from Buddhist influences as early as 538, and the "rationalistic" mode of Confucian ideology adapted from China.[3]

Confucianism has become a moral code of the Japanese, emphasizing personal virtue, justice, and devotion to the family. Two Confucian concepts, namely, subordination to one's superior (*chu*) and filial piety (*ko*), continue to pervade the minds of Japanese today and to influence their social institutions. Nevertheless, Japan's religious and ideological orientation has come to be conceived of as a distinctive ethos in which both tradition and modernity coexist without contradiction.

EUROPEANIZATION

The second phase of Japanese modernization began during the Meiji Restoration (1868) when Japan enthusiastically absorbed Western civilization, mainly from Great Britain, Germany, and France. *Wakon yosai* (Western learning and Japanese spirit) was the slogan adopted by the people at that time. The "Europeanization" of Japan during this period was so extensive that various spheres of Japanese society—governmental, political and legal systems, the army and navy, the system of education, and even manners, customs, and habits—experienced some degree of Westernization. Even the centuries-old tradition of Chinese medicine was replaced by German practices. The phrase *wayo secchu* emerged to describe the coexistence of Japanese and Western lifestyles. *Yofuku* (Western-style clothing) became fashionable over the *kimono* or *wafuku* (Japanese-style clothing). Men's traditional hairstyles (*chonmage*) and sword bearing were formally prohibited. Similarly, women chose to adopt Western hairstyles over their traditional *Nihongami* (Japanese hairstyles). Vegetarian and fish-eating Japanese began to eat meat and dairy products. Even in their living quarters, *yoma* (Western-style rooms) with Western-style furniture were incorporated into Japanese-style housing.

One of the few areas in which Japan remained independent of Western influence during this time was with regard to the institution of the family. Despite the modernization of lifestyles and many other spheres of Japanese society, *ie* (the traditional family system), which had previously existed only among the upper class, was codified and enforced throughout Japan regardless of social status.

Fortunately, perhaps, the Japanese zeal to imitate everything Western was later replaced with a reaction against Westernization, and many practices unworthy of imitation were discarded. What is most characteristic about Japan's effort to learn from the West is its spirit of independence in incorporating only those elements that would be advantageous to it. Japan succeeded in keeping its ethos and cultural-spiritual traditions intact while assimilating Western knowledge and technology. Thus, Japanese society today has retained its hybrid culture of tradition and modernity.

AMERICANIZATION

The third and final phase of Japan's modernization occurred after World War II. As a result of its defeat in the war and the subsequent seven-year occupation by Allied forces, Japan underwent total democratization, or Americanization, to be precise. The Japanese people spontaneously and enthusiastically supported the institutional reforms and new social systems implemented under the occupation, including political reform, equal rights for women, coeducation, and abolition of the traditional family system, to name a few. Enjoying the full support of the Japanese people, occupation authorities were able to implement these changes with astonishing rapidity. In yet another example of self-colonization, however, Japan adopted from America only those practices from which it would clearly benefit. As a result, Japan has become one of the world's leading nations while still maintaining its own identity and culture.

RESULTS OF JAPAN'S MODERNIZATION

Throughout the various stages of its modernization, Japan's strength has been in its ability to synthesize and internalize various contrasting social systems and cultural orientations. The coexistence of both tradition and modernity is the essence of the complex nature of modern-day Japan.

Figure I–1 illustrates the essence of the dual structural perspective of Japanese society today where modern Western capitalism is incorporated into a traditional agrarian society. The contrasting elements of external modernity and internal tradition coexist in a single system, composed of two layers and resulting in a dual structure. Underlying this structural duality is a complex of cultural assumptions—some modern and some traditional, some borrowed and some uniquely Japanese—that determines the manners and customs of the Japanese people, including regional variations, patterns of the working population, religion, and national character.

REGIONAL VARIATIONS

Cultural dichotomy by region—northeast versus southwest—has a long history in Japan, going as far back as the Kamakura period. Dichotomous regional variations account not only for differences in folklore and customs, blood type, fingerprints, and eating habits but also for patterns in intracommunity relationships. In the northeastern region, the binding force of the community is the hierarchical-vertical relationship among members, whereas in the southwestern region, horizontal-egalitarian relations are the norm.

Modern Japan has witnessed an excessive degree of urbanization in its metropolitan areas, accompanied by an equally excessive diminution of population (or *kaso*) in certain rural districts, particularly areas such as Kyushu, Tohoku, Hokkaido, and Chugoku where economic and in-

Figure I–1
A Dual Structural Model of Japanese Society

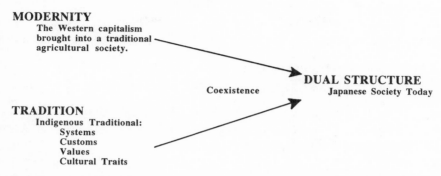

MODERNITY
  The Western capitalism
  brought into a traditional
  agricultural society.

Coexistence

DUAL STRUCTURE
Japanese Society Today

TRADITION
  Indigenous Traditional:
      Systems
      Customs
      Values
      Cultural Traits

dustrial activities have stagnated. Two striking demographic characteristics are evidenced in these *kaso* areas: acute attrition of children
between zero and fourteen years of age (from 35.9 percent in 1960 to
19.3 percent in 1985); and a dramatic increase in the numbers of elderly
(from 7.0 percent in 1960 to 17.2 percent in 1985).[4] In 1990, only about
6 percent of the total Japanese population resided in half the entire land
mass.[5]

This imbalance of population distribution may at least partially account for the duality of Japan's modern social structure. Ultramodern
urban living presents a sharp contrast to the traditional, rural lifestyles
that a small segment of Japanese society is still obliged to lead.

WORKING POPULATION

Changes in the pattern of Japan's working population have naturally
accompanied the modernization process (see Figure I–2). Until the early
1950s, approximately half of the Japanese working population was engaged in primary industries. Following the onset of the high economic
growth period in 1964, however, this proportion declined significantly;
it has now become less than 10 percent of the total working population.
In contrast, the proportion of tertiary industry workers has doubled from
the prewar period.

Significant attrition in Japan's farming population and households is
also evident. At 18 million (or 6.2 million households) in 1950, the
numbers fell to 13.9 million in 1960 and 3.9 million in 1990[6] (see Figure
I–3). In three decades, the Japanese farming population has been reduced

Figure I-2
Changes in Labor Force Participation Rate by Industry: 1920–1992

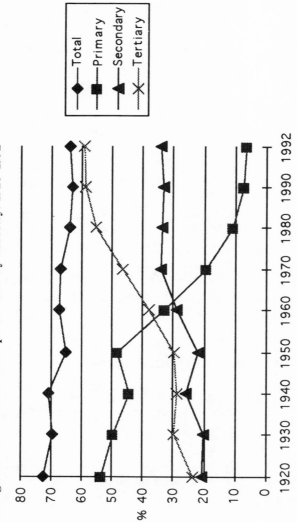

Primary industries include agriculture, forestry, and fishing.

Secondary industries include mining, construction, and manufacturing.

Tertiary industries include wholesale and retail trade, finance and insurance, real estate, transportation and communication, electric power, gas, and water supply, service industries, and public service.

Sources: Somucho Tokeikyoku, *Kokusei Chosa Hokoku* (Statistical Bureau of the Prime Minister's Office, National Census Report of the census conducted October 1 of the referent year), reported in the Institute of Population Problems, 1993a, 105, table 8–5; and statistics for 1992 were from the Asahi Shimbun, 1993, 97.

Figure I-3
Changes in the Farm Household Proportion by the Type of Participation: 1941–1990

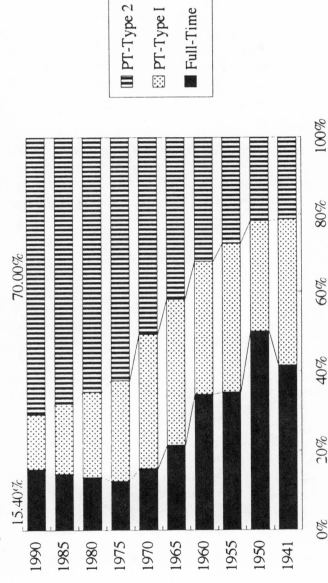

Sources: Norinsuisan-sho Tokei-hyo (Ministry of Agriculture, Forestry, and Fishing, Statistical Tables): 1941: *Noji Tokei Kaki Chosa* (Agricultural Statistics, Summer Survey); 1950, 1960, 1970, and 1980: *Sekai Noringyo Census* (World Census of Agriculture and Forestry); 1955: *Noka Chosa* (Farm Household Survey); 1965, 1975, and 1985: *Nogyo Census* (Agricultural Census); 1988: *Nogyo Chosa* (Agricultural Survey); 1990: *Nogyo Census* (Agricultural Census of Statistics and Information Department, Economic Affairs Bureau, Ministry of Agriculture, Forestry and Fisheries), reported in the *Japan Statistical Yearbook,* 1991, 152–153, tables 5–3, 5–4, and 5–5.

to one fifth of the pre–high economic growth period, indicating the emergence of dramatic structural change in modern Japanese society.

The introduction of modern technology into farming as well as insufficient levels of income have contributed to a sharp decline in the number
of full-time farmers and a rapid increase in the part-time farming population. Part-time farming households fall into two categories: In Type
1, the primary source of income is agriculture; in Type 2, it is nonagri-
culture. Since 1960, farm families have been shifting to Type 2. In 1990,
in a typical rural farming area in Japan, 15.4 percent of total farm households were full-time; 13.8 percent were part-time Type 1; and 70.7 percent were part-time Type 2[7] (see Figure I–3).

The reality of farm families today represents the dual structure of
Japanese society. Classified as engaging in the traditional farming occupation, these families actually rely on modern-type occupations for
their subsistence. These contrasting elements of modernity and tradition
coexist within the Japanese farming institution without conflict.

RELIGION

Despite the extensive influence of Chinese civilization, Japan has
maintained a distinctive multireligious cultural orientation that incorporates a variety of religious beliefs. Indeed, most Japanese view themselves as both Buddhists and Shintoists, and Japanese households
typically contain two separate altars for these devotions. Of Japan's 124
million people, 106 million say they believe in Shintoism, and 96 million
espouse Buddhism, obviously a double counting in religious orientation.
By contrast, there are only 1.5 million Christians in Japan and many
fewer Muslims and Jews.[8]

Literally meaning "the way of god," Shinto is the earliest and only
indigenous religion of Japan. Unconcerned with the problem of afterlife,
Shinto emphasizes the veneration of nature, purity, and everyday family
life. The Japanese today adopt Shinto rituals to celebrate major life
events, such as weddings, baptisms, the well-being of children, and the
construction of homes and buildings.

Buddhism, which first came to Japan in the year 538, is principally
concerned with life after death and the salvation of the individual. Growing out of this religious orientation, the Japanese people developed a
strong sense of ancestor worship. Thus, many of the Buddhist rituals
practiced today are organized in conjunction with the afterlife, such as

funerals and ancestor worship at the time of the vernal and the autumnal equinox and the *obon* festival in the summer.

Confucianism has become a moral code of the Japanese, emphasizing personal virtue, justice, and devotion to the family, including the spirit of one's ancestors. Two Confucian concepts have consistently been stressed in Japanese formal education, namely, *chu* (subordination to the emperor or superior) and *ko* (filial piety)—a philosophical orientation that persists in the minds of the Japanese today.

Christianity was brought to Japan by the Jesuit missionaries in 1549 and then banned during the Edo era. Under the Meiji Restoration, however, the Protestant ethic was reintroduced by various sojourners in Japan. As a result, Christianity has contributed to the modernization of Japan and is often regarded as a modern way of thought. Today, its adherents are less than 2 percent of the total population, divided fairly evenly between Protestants and Catholics.

NATIONAL CHARACTER AND HUMAN RELATIONS

Japan is more racially and ethnically homogeneous than almost any other modern nation. In fact, less than 1 percent of the total Japanese population is composed of non-Japanese nationals.[9] As others have recognized, this national homogeneity may be one of the primary reasons why the Japanese have been able to modernize their society and yet preserve a distinct sense of their own special identity.[10]

Japan's national character is defined by a unique set of human relations and a special code of human conduct. First, Japanese are socialized to value "groupism" over "individualism"; the welfare of the group as a whole is always given priority over the well-being of any one individual. Interhuman dynamics of the *oyabun-kobun* (superior-subordinate) and *sempai-kohai* (senior-junior) relationships illustrate the vertical orientation of Japanese society in which the interdependency of the group can simultaneously permit loyalty from subordinates and protection from the superior. [11]

Groupism also accounts for the Japanese style of bottom-up decision making. The essence of this style is the group-oriented and consensus-seeking process, which requires all parties to be in agreement with a decision before any major course of action is officially proposed.

Second, Japanese society is conformist. People care very much about how they are viewed by others and if they are following the accepted social norms in the prescribed fashion. Thus, we find that the working hours of the Japanese salaryman are notoriously long, and they have fewer holidays in comparison with full-time employees of other industrialized nations of the world. In 1990, for example, Japanese employees in the manufacturing sector worked an average of 2,124 hours per year and had 118 holidays. In contrast, American workers put in 1,948 hours and had 139 holidays.[12] To be treated as an insider, the Japanese salaryman must contribute to the work ethic, and therefore the cohesiveness of the group, by spending an inordinate amount of time in work-related activities.

Japan is perhaps best viewed as an "age-cracy," where one's major life events (i.e., entrance into college, employment, marriage, and childbearing) must take place at a certain age or else one falls off the golden path of social acceptability.

Third, Japan's racial and ethnic homogeneity have contributed to a mode of non-expressive, "high-context" communication in which the spoken word is often less important than nonverbal communication skills.[13] These include eye contact, *ishin denshin* (mind-to-mind communication), and facial expressions. There are also a number of high-context Japanese values, such as *amae*, *giri* and *on*, which have no meaningful English-language equivalent.[14] These words are derived from one's dependent and interdependent relations to others as a member of a group, rather than as an individual, and reflect the deep concern of the Japanese for harmonious human relations within the group.

Fourth, implicitness and indirectness are valued over explicitness and straightforwardness. This tendency toward ambiguity is perhaps best evidenced in the Japanese language itself, which shows no distinctions between singular/plural or gender and does not use definite/indefinite particles or pronouns. Even the syntax of the language (subject + object + verb) forces the listener to wait until the end of the sentence to understand the actor's behavior.

Americans often accuse Japanese of not saying a clear yes or no when, in reality, their actions have already clearly expressed a specific sentiment not allowed in words. The concepts of *tatemae* and *honne* perhaps best illustrate this dilemma. These words are used together by Japanese to describe the oft-encountered situation in which a person's stated reasons (*tatemae*) differ from his real intention, motive, or feeling (*honne*).[15]

Fifth, the Japanese socialization process tends to perpetuate a hierarchical-vertical structure of human relations, despite the constitutional equality of the people and their group orientation. Formal behavior patterns and honorific language forms clearly reflect this hierarchical orientation of Japanese culture. Anyone who has ever attempted to learn Japanese will appreciate the critical relationship between the honorific forms of the Japanese language (i.e., expressions showing respect, expressions demeaning oneself, and polite expressions) and the continued importance of hierarchy in Japanese society.

Sixth, perhaps as a by-product of the hierarchical orientation of human relations, is the behavioral reserve of the Japanese people. Candid expressions of one's feelings and the ability to quickly establish friendships are alien to the Japanese culture. At the same time, however, friendships with Japanese tend to be deep and long lasting.

In the professional arena, this cautious feeling-out process of the Japanese is epitomized in *nemawashi*, which literally means the gentle turning around of roots before transplanting a tree. By making every effort to achieve an informal agreement from all parties concerned before formally presenting a proposal, they obviate the possibility of direct personal conflict, which they find antithetical to the Japanese cultural assumption of group harmony.

Others have written extensively on many of these important aspects of Japan, but it is the deep-rooted traditions inherent in Japan's hierarchical family system that go farthest in explaining the meaning of contemporary Japanese society. As one of the most fundamental institutions in any society, the retention of Japan's traditional family system into the postwar period has had an important and lasting impact on attitudes and human relations in Japan, particularly in such areas as family and family dynamics, lifestyles, the education of children, the socialization of youth, women in the workplace, and the elderly. It is precisely these areas of Japanese society to which we now turn.

NOTES

1. Suzuki, 1993, 5.
2. Christopher, 1983, 39.
3. Kitagawa, 1983, 293.
4. National Land Agency, Office of Population Problems, 1994, 29, figure 2–8. Of the total Japanese population in 1985, the proportion of children between zero and fourteen years of age was 21.5 percent, and that of the elderly 65 years and over was 10.3 percent.
5. Ibid., 15, table 2–1. For additional discussions of regional variations in Japan, see Gamo (1960), Shimizu (1992), and Sofue (1971).

6. Institute of Population Problems, 1993a, 107, table 8–7.
7. Ministry of Agriculture, Agriculture Census, 1990, 11, table 3.
8. Agency for Cultural Affairs, 1992, reported in Asahi Shimbun, 1993, 255.
9. Institute of Population Problems, 1993a, 22, table 2–2.
10. Christopher, 1983, 39.
11. Nakane, 1970.

12. Ministry of Labor, *White Paper on Labor*, 1992, reported in Asahi Shim-bun, 1993, 99. "In the five-year program to make Japan a lifestyle power, adopted by the cabinet in June 1992, the government set a new target of reducing the total working hours per person to 1,800 hours per year by the end of the fiscal year 1996. The actual number of working hours in 1992 was 1,972 hours, 44 hours less than the previous year's actual and below the 2,000 hours level for the first time. This was due mainly to the fact that one-time work decreased as a result of the recession" (Asahi, 1993,99). Therefore, with the recovery of the Japanese economy, it is likely that the actual number of working hours of a Japanese worker will once again exceed the 2,000 hours level.

13. Hall and Hall, 1987.
14. Doi, 1971.
15. Doi, 1985. Additional pair-word usages include *soto* (outside) versus *uchi* (inside), and *omote* (the front) versus *ura* (the back).

PART I

THE JAPANESE FAMILY—CHANGE AND CONTINUITY

CHAPTER 1

Changes in the Japanese Family System

The basis of the contemporary Japanese family rests upon the feudal concept of *ie*, which may be translated as "stem family." More specifically, *ie* is defined as "a vertically composite form of nuclear families, one from each generation"[1] or a "series of first sons, their wives and minor children."[2] At the same time, *ie* means the household characterized as a corporate body of coresidents, each performing his or her role to maintain it. The coresidential and functional aspects of *ie* distinguishes it from other definitions of family, and their impact has extended to all aspects of family dynamics in Japan.

This feudal family structure came into existence during the Edo era among the upper strata of Japanese society, that is, aristocrats, the shogunate (lords) and samurai warriors. Under the *ie* system, the continuation of the family line from one generation to another depended upon the existence of male offspring in the family.

During this period, there was no *ie* system among the lower classes of Japanese society—peasants, artisans, merchants, or *eta* (the class of untouchables). Although all except *eta* had names, these were not family names but names given to indicate their occupations. In this context, the family was a functional unit defined by its economic activities. All of these classes engaged in economic production, and family members included not only blood relatives but also tenants and servants. Succession to the head of the family was not restricted to the eldest son. In order to guarantee succession, each family selected a son of superior ability, either from among the male offspring or by adopting another man from outside the family line, such as a son-in-law.

Even though the Meiji Restoration in 1868 ended the feudal era in Japan, it was only after enforcement of the Civil Code in 1898 that the class system was officially abolished, and the Japanese people were united as one under the emperor. In consequence, the *ie* system came to characterize both upper- and lower-class families, with each family directly subordinate to the emperor. Thus, the Meiji Restoration strengthened the hierarchical nature of the traditional Japanese family rather than modernizing it.

As had been the case among the upper-class families during the feudal period, the revised *ie* system transferred the household headship only to the eldest son. Moreover, succession to the headship also came to signify the inheritance of family assets and property. The family was no longer a unit of production and/or consumption characterized by egalitarian family relationships, as it had been among the lower-class families. Instead, the family structure shifted to a hierarchical-vertical organization comprising the ruler and the ruled.

Confucianism was adopted as the moral code of the Japanese and was propagated through education. It emphasized two major concepts: *chu* (loyalty and subordination to the emperor) and *ko* (filial piety). These two concepts molded the *ie* system and contributed to solidify the hierarchical-vertical orientation of human relationships within the structure.

With the enactment of the new Civil Code in 1947 after World War II, the family system in Japan underwent drastic change. In addition, Article 24 of the Constitution explicitly called for the safeguarding of the dignity of the individual and the equality of the sexes in family life. The *ie* system was abolished by the revised Civil Code, and the family unit was defined to include only husband, wife, and children. With the abolition of the household headship, husband and wife were given equal rights in the family. In addition, the family of a married son and his parents' family became independent of each other, and both were accorded equal positions in the larger family context. Thus, the Civil Code of 1947 can be regarded as an important modernizing element in the history of the Japanese family.

In reality, however, the stated ideals of equality and independence in the family have never been fully realized. Legislative change does not necessarily impact everyday life, and many of the unique aspects of the *ie* family system continue to pervade Japanese family and society. Thus, it is well to note that the Japanese family system today may not be truly modern; it contains elements of both tradition and modernity. These elements become apparent as we analyze three important aspects of the Japanese family: (1) the historical development of structural characteristics of the Japanese family; (2) the internal nature of the Japanese family and household; and (3) the regional variations in the Japanese family today.

STRUCTURAL CHARACTERISTICS OF THE FAMILY

There are seven structural characteristics that define family life in modern societies: the nuclear family, the three-generation family, family size, fertility behavior, age at first marriage and marriage patterns, divorce rates, the family life cycle.

The Nuclear Family

It is frequently asserted that industrialization and the nuclear family go hand-in-hand. What has been Japan's experience in this regard? According to the Census Bureau of Japan, a nuclear family is one that consists of a couple only, a couple with their unmarried children, or a single parent (either male or female) with unmarried children. Statistics reveal that the total proportion of all such nuclear households in Japan in 1920 was 54 percent. In the ensuing thirty-five years, the rate of increase was relatively gradual, and the proportion in 1955 was still slightly below 60 percent. Increasing to 61 percent in 1988, the proportion of nuclear households since then has been on a gradual decline, totaling just 59.5 percent in 1993, and projected to increase to only 60.6 percent by the year 2000 and to 62.3 percent by 2010.[3] Thus, contrary to popular references of the "nuclearization" of the modern Japanese household, there is no evidence of a striking increase in such households over the past seventy years.

The increased proportion of single-person households, on the other hand, has been dramatic indeed. Just 6.0 percent in 1920, single-person households had climbed to 24.5 percent in 1993. Combining the proportional changes of nuclear family and single-person households reveals an increase from 60 percent in 1920 to 84.0 percent in 1993. In other words, more than eight in every ten households in Japan today fall outside the traditional Japanese family system, clearly signaling the decline of the traditional stem family in Japan.

Future projections, however, suggest that the nuclear family may not become a universal phenomenon in the modern era. With nuclear households declining to 62.3 percent by the year 2010, the proportion of single-person households is expected to increase to 28.4 percent by that same year.[4] Thus, more than nine in every ten households in Japan will be of the nontraditional stem family type by the early part of the next century.

The rapid nuclearization of the Japanese family has been accentuated by the movement of young newlyweds, especially in urban areas, to households outside the family home. While upper-class families with ample property customarily extend financial support to their newlywed children by building detached homes on their premises, due to their lack of financial resources, people in the middle and lower classes are usually obliged to rent independent housing.[5] This might be the reason why we see an increase in the couple-only category of the nuclear family household.

Establishing a first residence outside the family home has yet to become a standard arrangement among newly married Japanese. In rural areas, most newlywed couples continue to reside with one of the couple's parents. Even in urban areas, many self-employed newlyweds still reside with the family of the eldest son, as long as space permits. But the shortage of housing space is so acute in urban areas that the nuclearization of reduced-sized families has increased in recent years.[6]

Surprisingly, however, the proportion of nuclear family households in the Tokyo metropolitan area has declined over the past twenty years, in 1990 coming in below the national average of 59.7 percent at 55.3 percent.[7] Prefectures adjacent to Tokyo, such as Saitama (66.4 percent), Kanagawa (62.9 percent), and Chiba (63.7 percent), have proportions of nuclear family households that are among the highest in all Japan. These southern districts of Kanto are regarded as Tokyo's satellite prefectures, where residents commute daily to the city. Thus, according to 1990 census data, the proportion of Tokyo's daytime population was 123.1 percent that of its actual residents, as opposed to 84.9 percent for Saitama, 86.0 percent for Chiba, and 89.4 percent for Kanagawa.[8]

Another point to be noted concerning household structures in Tokyo is that the proportion of single-person households amounted to slightly

more than one third of the total households in 1990 (35.9 percent in Tokyo versus 23.1 percent for the national average). This proportion is naturally much lower in rural areas where the proportion of nuclear family households is also low. In Yamagata, for example, only 14.6 percent of all households were of the single-person variety, and 45.2 percent were nuclear; in Toyama, the proportions were 14.3 percent and 50.8 percent, respectively.[9] Clearly, the nuclearization of Japanese households in urban settings has been progressing much faster than that in rural regions.

A cursory examination of the distribution of couple-only nuclear households by region and by age reveals that the majority in rural areas have members aged sixty years and over (56.6 percent as opposed to 48.0 percent in large cities), while only a fraction have members below age thirty (3.8 percent in rural areas and 9.9 percent in large cities).[10] Thus, the recent increase in nuclear family households may in fact be due not to the increase in newlyweds moving outside the home but rather to the increase in elderly-couple-only households. Likewise, it is reasonable to assume that nuclear family households in rural areas are those of couples with unmarried children rather than the couple-only type.

The Three-Generation Family

Just as the nuclear family is concomitant with modernization, the stem family (also referred to as the three-generation family or simply the generational family) seems to be one of the preconditions for modern economic development. The stem family structure incorporates a support network for elder members in the household, where three, four, or even five generations coreside in a single household.

The nuclearization of the Japanese family becomes more apparent when we analyze changes in the proportion of three-generation families in Japan. Slightly more than one third of all Japanese households in 1955 (37.5 percent), and one in every five households in 1965 (19.2 percent), today the stem family accounts for as few as one in every seven households (13.1 percent in 1992).[11]

Of Japan's total households in 1992, those with elder members aged sixty-five years and over constituted slightly more than a quarter, or 28.8 percent of the total. Of these elderly, only one third reside in three or more generational households (86.8 percent in 1960 versus 36.6 percent in 1992). In addition, households with elder members only have in-

creased dramatically over the years. The proportion of single-person elderly households increased from 5.9 percent in 1960 to 15.7 percent in
1992. Similarly, the proportion of elderly-couple-only households increased from 8.3 percent in 1960 to 22.8 percent in 1992, and they will
constitute more than one third (35.9 percent) by the year 2010.[12]

Clearly, a greater proportion of three-generation households in Japan
now compose elderly-only and/or elderly-couple-only households, and
an increasing number of Japanese elderly today are obliged to adopt
independent lifestyles, not concomitant with the traditional stem family
system.

Family Size

Given this growth of nontraditional family structures, it is not surprising to find that the total number of Japanese households has nearly
quadrupled over the past seven decades, from 11 million in 1920 to 42.4
million in 1993, and will increase to as many as 50.2 million in 2010.
In contrast, the number of family members in one household has decreased dramatically.[13] The average family in prewar Japan had more
than 5 members, but today it has less than 3 (2.99 in 1992), and by the
year 2010, average family size will be as small as 2.73. This increase in
the total number of households and the decrease in average family size
signal the emergence of the modern family in Japan.

Fertility Behavior

The noticeable attrition in the size of the Japanese family suggests a
decline in the fertility rate among Japanese women today. Since World
War II, in fact, the fertility rate among Japanese women has been in
sharp decline—the 5.1 rate in 1925 dropped to an average of 4.5 in the
1930s, 4.3 in the 1940s, 3.0 in the 1950s. Falling below the population
maintenance level in the 1960s, it bottomed out at 1.57 in 1989, bringing
the so-called 1.57 shock in Japan. Most recent statistics reveal an amaz-
ingly low fertility rate of 1.50 in 1992.[14]

This extremely low rate of fertility among Japanese women is having
a significant impact on various spheres of socioeconomic life in Japan,
generating such serious problems as zero population growth (the repro-

duction level is 2.1), a decline in the labor force population, the coming of an aging society, and welfare programs.

Japanese married women who do not bear children compose two contrasting groups: those who do not want to bear children and those who are unable to do so. All in all, however, one of the major reasons for this remarkably low fertility rate is that Japanese women are delaying marriage.

Age at First Marriage and Patterns of Spouse Selection

In 1882 the average age at first marriage for Japanese men was 22.10 years, and for women, 19.04 years.[15] One hundred years later in 1992, the average age was 28.4 for men and 26.0 for women,[16] among the highest of all industrialized nations. It is interesting to note, however, that Japanese men in prewar Japan married later than they do today. Thus, with women marrying considerably later than they did before, the age gap between spouses has shrunk from 3.9 years in 1908 to 2.4 years in 1992. The improved status of women in Japanese society has led, perhaps, to a new perspective on marriage, one that views marriage as a companionship between equals in which the ages of the spouses are closer.

Marriage is almost universal in Japan. According to the 1990 census, of people seventy-five years and over, only 0.8 percent of men and 1.4 percent of women were never married. Most men marry before the age of fifty (93.3 percent in 1990) and women before the age of forty (92.5 percent in 1990).[17] This is not at all specific to the Japanese population but holds true across many industrialized Western societies.[18] However, the situation in Japan is outstanding. Many people in Japan's age-cratic society still feel that they have to follow specific patterns of behavior at designated periods in their lives, regardless of personal preference.

Proportions of never-married people in higher age brackets, however, have been increasing dramatically over the last twenty years. In 1992, never-married Japanese men between the ages of twenty-five and twenty-nine, thirty and thirty-four, and thirty-five and thirty-nine were 64.4 percent, 32.6 percent, and 19.0 percent, respectively, increases of as much as 20 percent since 1972. Rates of Japanese women between the ages of twenty and twenty-four and twenty-five and twenty-nine who had never married were 85.0 percent and 40.2 percent, respectively, pronounced increases of 13.4 percent and 22.1 percent between 1972 and

1992.[19] These statistics confirm that Japanese men and women have been delaying their marriages considerably more than their Western counterparts.[20]

Clearly, both the concept of, and the attitude toward, marriage has changed significantly in Japan. Under the traditional *ie* system, the prime reason for marriage was the continuation of the family line, and the will of the parents played an important role in a couple's decision to marry. During the war period, for example, approximately 70 percent of all marriages in Japan were arranged by the parents. Today, on the other hand, marriage is based on mutual consent, and the couple's wishes are given priority over those of the parents. Love marriages now constitute as many as 83 percent of all marriages in Japan and are especially pronounced in urban areas.[21]

It is interesting to note the strong correlation between arranged marriage and age; the higher the age of a husband or wife at first marriage, the more likely it is that the marriage is arranged. Both men and women who had arranged marriages met their spouses, were engaged, and then married much later than those who had love marriages. As expected, the period from the initial meeting to the marriage for the arranged-marriage group was less than a year, whereas it was more than three years for the love-marriage group.[22] Today arranged marriages are particularly exceptional in young marriages of women below twenty years and men below twenty-five years.

Over the past two decades, ages for the initial encounter of Japanese men and women have been quite stable (1972–1977: 24.91 years for men; 22.29 years for women; 1987–1992: 25.24 years for men; 22.59 years for women). Therefore, the major reason for the delayed marriage of Japanese women today can be attributed to the prolonged period preceding their actual marriage, which increased from 1.97 years for newly married couples between 1972 and 1977 to 2.97 years for those between 1987 and 1992.[23] Thus, over the past 15 years, this period has increased 1 full year. While the increased incidence of love marriage seems indicative of a more modern attitude toward marriage and family among Japanese young people, this longer premarital phase suggests that traditional attitudes about the importance of the marriage contract remain—further evidence of the dual structure of modernity and tradition operating within Japan's fundamental social institutions.

Divorce

In general, divorce occurs more frequently in Western societies than in Japan mainly because Japanese view divorce as a termination of relations not only between husband and wife but between parent and child as well. Given the continued importance of the family in Japan, husbands and wives are more willing to sacrifice their individual happiness for what they deem to be the overall welfare of the family.

Nevertheless, in the decade between 1963 and 1983, the divorce rate in Japan rose from 0.74 to 1.51. This increase was followed by a downward trend: In 1984, for the first time in twenty years, the divorce rate decreased by 0.01 from its postwar high of 1.51, and by 1988, it had dropped to 1.26. More recently, however, the divorce rate has once again shown signs of increase, rising to as high as 1.53 in 1993.[24] Reasons for this renewed upward trend are not clear, although it may be a sign that more Japanese women have come to value independent living over the traditional marriage structure. In contrast, the U.S. divorce rate continues to decline: down to 4.7 in 1993 from 5.3 in 1981.[25] Although the exact reasons for this decline have yet to be identified, it is generally believed that Americans' views of matrimony have entered a more conservative phase. The stalled U.S. economy may also be contributing to the decline in divorce.

In the case of Japan, the discernable trend toward the lengthening of marriage prior to divorce can be explained by the fact that more marriages are now being made for personal reasons rather than considerations of family lineage and family harmony. Under the latter circumstances, if divorce is to occur, it usually does so relatively soon after marriage, the time when decisions on children are made. But in cases where marriage is motivated by considerations of personal happiness, divorce may occur at any time.

Most divorces in Japan now occur more than five years after the start of the marriage, and the average duration of marriage prior to divorce is almost ten years.[26] Compared to 1947, when 61 percent of all divorces occurred within the first five years of marriage, in 1992 these early divorces accounted for just 38.2 percent of the total. Increased divorce among couples married for over twenty years is especially pronounced: 3.1 percent in 1947 versus 15.4 percent in 1992.[27]

Japanese attitudes toward divorce have clearly changed over the years. When asked whether or not dissatisfaction with a spouse makes divorce an acceptable option, 26.8 percent of married women in 1982 answered affirmatively and 59.3 percent negatively.[28] After only one decade, these percentages changed to 44.6 percent and 43.5 percent, respectively.[29]

Family Life Cycle

Over the last century, dramatic changes have occurred in the Japanese family life cycle, bringing the overall life cycle pattern of Japanese women in line with that of their American and Canadian counterparts.[30] The modernization trends described above, in combination with the expanded life expectancy of the Japanese people, have made life in Japanese society today not so different from life in other advanced industrialized Western nations.

INTERNAL CHARACTERISTICS OF THE FAMILY

Changing internal and attitudinal dimensions of the Japanese family also play a large part in defining the character of life in Japan today.

Family Dynamics

Modern Japanese family dynamics are by no means as hierarchical-vertical as those found in the traditional *ie* system. They still maintain, however, a distinct vertical orientation. Analyses of filial violence in Japan reveal two important patterns of family interaction: unintegrated conjugal relationships and the psychological absence of the father in the family. The continued lack of spousal integration, or real companionship between husband and wife, is symptomatic of traditional family life in Japan, and it leads to unbalanced relations within the family.

The nuclearization of the Japanese family has resulted in strong intergenerational ties between a mother and her children. With the introduction of advanced technology into everyday life, the Japanese housewife and mother has been left with a great deal of spare time, most of which she devotes to child rearing. As a result, many Japanese mothers today are overprotective of and overindulgent with their children.

Frantically education minded, mothers often pay less attention to the emotional nurturing of their children.

The status of Japanese fathers has deteriorated significantly since World War II; they are no longer the authoritarian figure in the home. Mothers compensate for frustrations with their spouses by intensifying the already close-knit ties with their children, reflecting the vertical generational ties of the traditional *ie* system. Sometimes this mother-child relationship becomes so intense that Japanese mothers conceive of their children as their own personal property.

Thus, nuclearization of the Japanese family has reconfirmed the strong vertical ties found in the traditional *ie* system, rather than building the strong horizontal husband-wife relationships that are found in Western societies. Although Japanese legislation upholds the principles of egalitarianism in the family, the stated ideals of equality and independence have not yet been fully realized. The essence of the traditional family system persists in modern Japanese society, where the purpose of the institutional family is to raise children and to fulfill a social and economic function in society, rather than to provide companionship, affection, and happiness for all family members.

The Modified Stem Family

In Japan, nearly 60 percent of the elderly aged sixty-five years and over live with their adult children, as compared to 30 percent in Western societies. This coresidency rate increases as the elderly get even older, rising to 50.3 percent for those between sixty-five and sixty-nine years, and 72.6 percent for those over eighty years.[31] Perhaps due to the immature nature of Japan's industrialization or the ingrained values of the Japanese family system, the majority of the Japanese elderly still adopt traditional coresidency living arrangements.

In light of this high coresidence situation, Japan's modern family system has been labeled a "modified stem" family.[32] Family members experience both the modern nuclear household and traditional stem family arrangements alternately throughout their life course. As Figure 1–1 illustrates, a typical Japanese woman will go through various family phases during her life course, but the family itself remains the same. This fluidity of the internal nature of the Japanese family structure allows for the coexistence of traditional and modern elements.

Figure 1–1
The Modified Stem Family in Japan

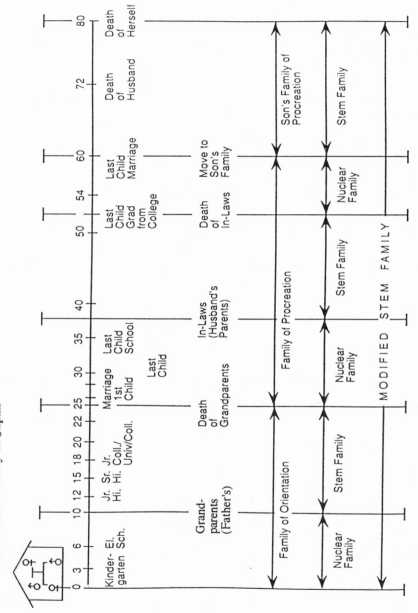

Source: Kumagai, 1986b, 379.

REGIONAL VARIATIONS

While national statistics clearly indicate the modernization of the Japanese family, important regional variations do exist, particularly with regard to marriage and divorce patterns.[33]

Today, marriages in Japan occur more frequently in urban areas than in rural settings, while divorces are more prevalent in urban areas and rural fishing villages than in rural farming regions. Japanese men and women in rural areas also tend to marry earlier and have more offspring than their urban counterparts. Thus, urbanization and industrialization lead to a nuclear family structure where small family size is optimal, fertility rates decline, and divorce increases. Generally speaking, members of urban nuclear households do not adhere to traditional values and mores as much as those in rural areas where the generational family system is prevalent. Therefore, married couples in urban nuclear households are less bound to unhappy marriages and more likely to pursue divorce than those in the rural-based traditional stem family households.[34] Clearly, there are regional variations in the Japanese family today, and two contrasting components, the modern and the traditional, can be traced in urban and rural settings, respectively.

Perhaps, then, it is best to describe the contemporary Japanese family structure as a modified stem family, which is modern externally and traditional internally and modern in urban settings and traditional in rural ones. The dual forces of tradition and modernity coexist within the institution of the Japanese family today.

NOTES

1. Morioka, 1967, 597; also see Lebra, 1984, 20.
2. E. Johnson, 1964, 839.
3. Statistical Bureau of the Ministry of Health and Welfare, 1993b, 9, table 2; Institute of Population Problems, 1993b, 8, table 1; Institute of Population Problems, 1993b.
4. Institute of Population Problems, 1993b, 8, table 1.
5. Fukutake, 1981, 120.
6. Ibid., 121.
7. Institute of Population Problems, 1993a, 163, table 12–24.
8. Ibid., 168, table 12–29.
9. Ibid., 163, table 12–24.

10. Statistical Bureau of the Ministry of Health and Welfare, 1989, 3, table 2.

11. Statistical Bureau of the Ministry of Health and Welfare, 1993b, 9, table 2.

12. Ibid., 14–15, tables 8 and 9; Institute of Population Problems, 1993b, 9, table 2.

13. Institute of Population Problems, 1993a; 81, table 7–1; 6, figures 1 and 2; 9, table 1; Statistical Bureau of the Ministry of Health and Welfare, 1993b, 8, table 1.

14. Kumagai, 1984a; Statistical Bureau of the Ministry of Health and Welfare, 1993, 6–7; Statistical Bureau of the Ministry of Health and Welfare, 1994, 4, table 2.

15. Prime Minister's Office, *Official Bulletin*, 1886.

16. Statistical Bureau of the Ministry of Health and Welfare, 1993a, 17, table 10; Prime Minister's Office, 1993, 4, table II–1–2.

17. Statistics Bureau of the Management and Coordination Agency, 1991, 13, table 4–3.

18. In modern industrialized Western societies, more than 90 percent of women marry at least once by forty years of age. Ibid., 13, Table 4–2.

19. Economic Planning Agency, 1992, 409, table I–2–3; Institute of Population Problems, 1993a, 81, table 6–23.

20. According to the *U.N. Demographic Yearbook of 1990*, in the United States, rates for never-married men in the twenty to twenty-four, twenty-five to twenty-nine, and thirty to thirty-four age brackets were 79.3 percent, 45.2 percent, and 27.0 percent, respectively. For women in the twenty to twenty-four, twenty-five to twenty-nine, and thirty to thirty-four age groups, these rates were 62.8 percent, 31.1 percent, and 16.4 percent, respectively. See United Nations, 1992. Statistics for Japanese counterparts for respective age groups for both men and women were all higher by approximately 20 percent, except for women in the thirty to thirty-four age group (13.9 percent). Institute of Population Problems, 1993a, 85, table 6-24.

21. Institute of Population Problems, 1993c, 4, table II–2–1. In a former survey conducted in 1987, the proportions of arranged and love marriages to all marriages were 23.6 percent and 73.8 percent, respectively; in urban areas: 22.3 percent versus 74.4 percent; and in rural areas: 25.5 percent versus 73.0 percent. In the most recent 1992 survey, proportions of arranged and love marriages to all marriages were 15.2 percent and 82.8 percent; in urban areas: 13.0 percent versus 85.1 percent; and in rural areas: 22.0 percent versus 75.9 percent.

22. Ibid., 5, table II–3–1.

23. Ibid., 6, table II–3–2.

24. Kumagai, 1983b, 1992a, 1992b; Statistical Bureau of the Ministry of Health and Welfare, 1994, 4, table 2.

25. U.S. Department of Health and Human Services, 1994; Center for Disease Control and Prevention, National Center for Health Statistics, 1994.

26. Statistical Bureau of the Ministry of Health and Welfare, 1991, 5, table 7.

27. Statistical Bureau of the Ministry of Health and Welfare, 1993a: 19, table 12.

28. Prime Minister's Office, 1992b.

29. Prime Minister's Office, 1992a.

30. Kumagai, 1984a.

31. Kumagai, 1992b, 7, table 8.

32. Nasu, 1962.

33. Kumagai, 1987a; 1992b.

34. For additional studies of rural-urban variations in the contemporary Japanese family, see Kumagai, 1987a; 1992b, 211–216.

CHAPTER 2

Popular Culture/Lifestyles of the Japanese Family

How are marriage and the family popularly perceived by Japanese people today? The images described below suggest an interesting mix of modern popular culture and the traditional values of feudal Japan.

MARRIAGE

Although the average age of first marriage for Japanese women rose to twenty-six years in 1992, twenty-five years is still considered a critical turning point in a woman's life. At twenty-five years of age, a Japanese women is called "a Christmas cake," something for which there is no use after the twenty-fifth. Despite the fact that Japanese women are marrying later, they still worry about missing the opportunity to marry once they pass the critical age of twenty-five.

More and more single women today have acquaintances with men even though they would never consider them as marriage partners. These young Japanese men are given various names, depending upon the nature and extent of the acquaintances, including *mitsugu-kun*, *tsukushinbo*, *asshi-kun*, and *keep-kun*.

A *mitsugu-kun* is a young man who spends all of his money on gifts and taking a girl out. *Tsukushinbo*, made up of *tsukusu* (being dedicated) and *bo* (a boy or a man), refers to a man who not only gives gifts but also does whatever his girl asks him. *Asshi-kun* comes from *ashi*, which means legs, feet, or vehicle in Japanese. This is a young man used by a girl as a chauffeur, giving rides at her convenience. A *keep-kun* is a man who is kept until the *honmei-kun*, or ideal marriage partner, comes along.

What does it take to be a *honmei-kun*? Such a man must possess attractive physical characteristics, the proper family background, and a high level of educational attainment. The Japanese word that signifies an ideal marriage partner is *sanko*, meaning high in three areas: height, educational background, and income.

It is not surprising, then, that many young Japanese men have difficulty meeting women who want to marry them. The Japanese phrase *tama no koshi* refers to the well-known Cinderella story where a poor servant girl falls in love with and marries a handsome prince. Recently, however, *gyaku tama*, or the reversal of the Cinderella story, is more popular. Young men in Japan are realizing how impossible it will be to become rich during their lifetime, so they are looking for the chance to marry a woman from a wealthy family.

COST OF GETTING MARRIED

The cost of getting married in Japan has become so high that it places an unbearable burden on Japanese young people. According to data compiled by Sanwa Bank, one of the leading private banks in Japan, the average cost of getting married in 1992 was ¥8.057 million ($80,570). This astronomically high sum is usually raised in the following manner: 24 percent through gifts, 40 percent from parents, and 37 percent by the couple themselves.[1] In other words, each couple that wants to marry must save as much as ¥3 million ($30,000).

Why is it so costly to marry? Japanese people used to have wedding receptions at home. After World War II, however, as space became more limited, hotels began to offer all-inclusive wedding packages. These wedding package programs have become a booming business for the hotel industry in Japan today. A wedding reception at a fashionable hotel in Tokyo can cost as much as ¥5.3 million ($53,000) for 100 guests, including a three-meter high wedding cake and four to five changes of clothes for the bride. After the wedding reception, most newlyweds go on a honeymoon. Of them, 85 percent go abroad, double the figure of ten years ago. The most popular honeymoon destinations in 1992 were Australia, Europe, and Bali in Indonesia. The average amount of money spent by a couple for a seven- to ten-day honeymoon was ¥1.5 million ($15,000).

FAMILY RELATIONS

Modern Japanese family relations are popularly described by a number of terms that derive from the Japanese word for family, or *kazoku*. *Zoku* refers to a clan or a group of people, and its various modern-day transformations include *lokku-zoku*, *chin-zoku*, *komori-zoku* and *rozu famili-zoku*. These terms offer an interesting and somewhat sad commentary on family life in Japan today.

- *Lokku-zoku* is a family in which the husband leaves home for work early in the morning, locking the door quietly after him so as not to awaken his wife. *Lokku* is Japanese English for "lock."
- *Chin-zoku* is a family in which members eat meals prepared in microwave ovens. When foods being prepared in a microwave are ready to be served, we hear the sound "chin."
- *Komori* in *komori-zoku* means the nocturnal bat. Japanese children today spend most of their time in school or "cramming" after school. At home, they are immersed in the *fami-con*, or home computer; rarely do they play outdoors. Thus, they are called *komori-zoku*.
- *Rozu famili-zoku* refers to the two separate flowers of a rose, known as *bara-bara* in Japanese. Today, members of the Japanese family are busy with their own individual pursuits: Fathers play golf, mothers enjoy karaoke, and children study. Their activities are *bara-bara*, since there is no integration of the family as a whole.

DUALITY OF LIFESTYLES

Class Identification

The Prime Minister's Office of Public Relations has been conducting annual public opinion surveys since 1958, including questions concerning the people's self-identification of their social standing. Since the initiation of the survey, the majority of Japanese have identified themselves as belonging to the middle class (72.4 percent in 1958; 90.0 percent in 1993). As Figure 2-1 illustrates, nine of every ten Japanese today identify themselves as belonging to the middle class—upper class: 1.2 percent; middle class: 90.0 percent (upper-middle: 11.1 percent; middle-middle: 54.6 percent; lower-middle: 24.3 percent); and lower class: 5.6 percent.

Japanese who identify themselves as belonging to the upper class have always been minimal (0.2 percent in 1958; 1.2 percent in 1993), whereas those who classify themselves in the lower class have declined dramatically, from 17 percent in 1958 to 5.6 percent in 1993.[2] But the middle-class identification of Japanese has always been overwhelming, perhaps epitomizing Japan's group-oriented culture.

Quality of Life

But how does the actual quality of life in Japan compare with the national wealth? Numerous public and private reports have recently indicated marked differences between the life quality of the average individual and the national level of economic success.[3] The key word used in most of these studies is *yutori*, a difficult word to translate into English but one that connotes latitude, leisurely mindedness, or free time. Echoing throughout Japan is the phrase *yutori aru seikatsuo*, indicating a strong desire on the part of Japanese to lead a more comfortable life than that to which they are accustomed. Now that the society as a whole has achieved a considerable level of economic affluence, people have come to realize the insufficiency in their life quality.[4]

THE EXTERNAL DIMENSION OF QUALITY OF LIFE

General Aspects

National income statistics revealed in GNP (gross national product) measures show the economic activities of a nation in abstract terms only. They provide a common basis for international comparison but do not tell much about the qualitative side of national livelihood. Understanding the actual changes that economic advancement has brought to people's lives in Japan requires a more careful examination of the various aspects of their lifestyle.

The National Standard Index (NSI) was developed by the Economic

Figure 2–1

Changes in the Rate of the Middle-Class Identification: 1958–1993

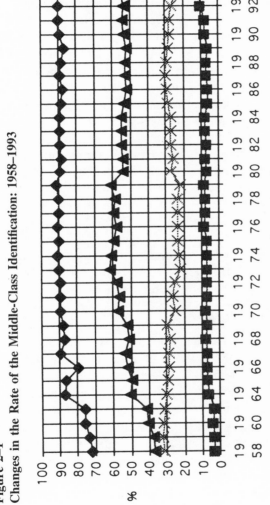

Source: Prime Minister's Office, 1993c, 39–43.

Planning Agency for just this purpose and has been administered every year since 1972.[5] Results of the 1993 NSI survey clearly reflect the impact of economic recession since the summer of 1991 and people's awareness about the rapid aging of the Japanese population.[6] The number of people who are satisfied with life in general has declined from 53.5 percent in 1990 to 51.9 percent in 1993.[7] Those with positive attitudes toward the future of Japanese society have also declined, from 46.2 percent to 37.9 percent over the same three-year period. Moreover, only slightly more than one fourth of the Japanese people view their old age positively, down from 29.2 percent in 1990 to 26.9 percent in 1993.[8] Clearly, the Japanese people are very much concerned about their lives in old age and place prime importance on issues relating to the social welfare of the elderly, including sufficient pensions (92.8 percent); living comfortably (91.8 percent); and well-developed social services for families with infirm or disabled elderly members (91.8 percent).[9]

Another recent government study reveals similar trends in the Japanese people's outlook on contemporary society, no doubt reflecting the prolonged economic recession, the acute shortage of rice, and uncertainty about the future.[10] Less than three in ten people believe that Japan is moving in a positive direction, while almost half (45.4 percent) consider Japan to be on a downward course—the highest proportion since 1971 when such questions were first incorporated in the study. There are also signs of a waning spiritual affluence and leisure-mindedness among Japanese people. A growing number of people describe Japanese society as dull (12.0 percent) and gloomy (5.9 percent).

A cross-cultural analysis of the NSI data, including Japan, the United States, the United Kingdom, Germany, France, and Sweden, reveals that Japan is above average in such fields as health, economic stability, environment and safety, and family life. Japan scores high on the health measurement because of its long life expectancy and low infant mortality rate; and low divorce rates and the low proportion of elderly living alone earn Japan high marks in the area of family life. Thus, Japanese living standards appear fairly well balanced and of relatively high quality.

In reality, however, life quality in Japan today has many negative features. The NSI data have Japan falling below average in community and social activities and learning and cultural activities. The average Japanese, for example, works more hours per year than his Western counterparts, housing space is insufficient, and infrastructures such as the sewage system remain at a substandard level.[11]

Household Budget and Living Expenditures

General living standards of the Japanese have improved significantly in recent years. The average monthly income for workers' households was ¥563,855 in 1992, a nominal increase of 2.7 percent over the previous year. Although the consumer price index for 1992 was nearly three times as high as that of 1970, monthly net income over the same period more than quadrupled, so that increases in the cost of living did not exceed increased rates of income.

Engel's coefficient, or the proportion of food costs to the total consumption expenditures of a household, is a useful indicator for the household budget condition. This proportion has declined significantly over the years, from nearly two fifths (39.8 percent) of the total consumption expenditure in 1959 to less than a quarter (23.7 percent) in 1992.[12]

It is interesting to note, too, that Japanese people have been purchasing more Western-style than traditional Japanese foodstuffs. Between 1963 and 1991, annual food purchases per household have changed as follows:[13]

Rice	372 to 122 kgs.
Fresh fish/shellfish	68.6 to 47.5 kgs.
Bread	32.1 to 39.7 kgs.
Beef	7.5 to 11.3 kgs.
Pork	7.1 to 16.8 kgs.
Chicken	3.1 to 12.9 kgs.
Milk	58 to 114 ltrs.
Cheese	0.36 to 1.83 kgs.
Margarine	0.79 to 2.59 kgs.

The cost of living in Japan is extremely high, surpassing that of most other Western industrialized societies. An international retail comparison indicates that prices for almost all foodstuffs and most other goods in Tokyo are the highest in the world, except for mass-produced goods such as tissue paper and for specialized services such as dry cleaning.[14]

When Japanese consumers in the greater metropolitan area were asked what they would do if their annual income decreased by 10 percent,[15] more than eight out of ten answered that they would conserve on household expenditures, more than four out of ten would take up part-time jobs to earn extra income (43 percent), and more than 15 percent, mostly those in their thirties with families, would move to rural areas if they could find jobs. Thus, a decrease in income can be expected to have a significant impact not only on consumer purchasing but also on the structure of modern Japanese society as a whole.

Consumer Durables

Consumer durables, the most visible sign of affluence, contribute to a more comfortable lifestyle. During the initial postwar period of Japanese reconstruction, the Three Sacred Treasures of the Imperial House, popularly known as *san shuno jinki*,[16] were electric washing machines, refrigerators, and vacuum cleaners. Later, the three sacred treasures became the 3C's, namely, cars, coolers (room air-conditioners), and color TV sets. Today, the Japanese people have turned to high-technology commodities and high-quality merchandise.

Of the thirty-eight major consumer durables listed in the Economic Planning Agency's March 1992 consumer survey, color TV sets, electric washing machines, refrigerators, and vacuum cleaners had reached a 100 percent saturation rate in all households.[17]

Housing

As of October 1, 1988, the total number of dwellings in Japan was 42,010,000, an 8.8 percent increase in the five-year period between 1983 and 1988, and triple the number of forty years ago. But since 1973, and in some periods previously, the number of households in Japan has exceeded that of dwellings. This gap has been continuously widening, attesting to the poor housing conditions of most Japanese.[18]

On the other hand, the number of rooms, their size (excluding unoccupied dwellings), and area space per house have all been increasing over the years, suggesting that the quality of housing in Japan has improved considerably,[19] and there has been a substantial increase in the rate of new construction.[20] But because the floor space per newly constructed house has not increased much, the quality of housing in Japan has not significantly improved.[21]

THE INTERNAL DIMENSION OF QUALITY OF LIFE

Despite the country's amazing economic growth, most Japanese continue to struggle daily with a high cost of living, cramped homes, and long working hours. Some believe that these problems represent an integral part of the Japanese lifestyle to which most Japanese have easily adjusted. High costs are justified since the quality of goods and services is also high. Homes may be small, but they are comfortable for the Japanese people, and long working hours are the choice of employees themselves.

Government reports on annual working hours contradict each other. According to the Ministry of Labor, average annual working hours for a Japanese person in 1992 were 2,095, slowly approaching the national target of 1,800 hours. These statistics are based on reports submitted to the ministry by Japanese corporations. Labor statistics completed by the Japan Management and Coordination Agency, however, show figures nearly 20 percent higher (2,506 working hours) for the same category. The Economic Planning Agency attributes this discrepancy to various forms of *zangyo* (onetime work), which are not officially reported to the corporations. These include *service zangyo* (overtime work without remuneration); *furoshiki zangyo* (wrapping up unfinished work); and *chukan kanrishoku zangyo* (onetime work by midlevel managers who are not qualified for onetime remuneration).[22] These forms of unpaid, overtime work most clearly result from the choices of Japanese workers themselves.

A propensity toward overwork seems to be ingrained in the national character of the Japanese people. In fact, a growing number of workers are reported to have died of *karoshi* (death due to the accumulation of fatigue caused by overwork). *Karoshi* is neither a medical nor an official term but a word popularized since 1982 by the Japanese mass media to symbolize the increase of workaholics in Japan.[23]

The exact origin of *karoshi* in Japan is unknown. It may have started as early as the 1960s with the onset of Japan's high economic growth period, then increased dramatically after the first oil shock in 1973. In any case, it was not until 1988 that the first privately funded agency (Dial 110 for *Karoshi*) was established in a law firm in Nagoya. Since its establishment, this agency alone has handled as many as 3,000 cases.

Symptoms of *karoshi* are typically cerebral hemorrhage or heart disease, and the patient dies within seven days of the onset of the illness.

Victims of *karoshi* are predominantly middle-aged men (94.3 percent), and 64 percent are between forty and fifty-nine years of age. Industries in which victims of *karoshi* can be found vary extensively, and while some victims are employed by organizations, others are self-employed store owners, for example.[24]

Today Japanese men and women have attained the world's highest life expectancy at birth, and most expect to live into their eighties. It is ironic, therefore, that Japanese middle-aged heads of households, many of whom are established leaders in Japanese society, are also the primary victims of *karoshi*. These men still adhere to the traditional ideology of dedication to work at the expense of one's personal life.

Yet the waning impact of tradition in favor of more modern lifestyles is observable among younger generations in Japan. One recent government survey reveals that seven out of ten people (72.1 percent) believe that Japanese men today place more emphasis on their home life than on their work. Responses are particularly high among people in the thirty to thirty-nine-year age bracket (79.5 percent for men; 86.0 percent for women).[25] Similar trends are also observable with regard to changing lifestyles. The majority of Japanese people (75.3 percent) believe it is desirable to focus more on family-related than work-related activities, a tendency that is especially pronounced among those in the thirty-six to thirty-nine-year age bracket (82.2 percent for men; 89.4 percent for women).[26] Nevertheless, surveys by the Prime Minister's Office reveal that most Japanese (69.8 percent) are generally satisfied with their present lives.[27] An investigation of the internal dimensions of life quality will help to determine if these positive attitudes are indicative of a truly affluent life.

Affluence Indices

In an attempt to analyze the level of affluence of the individual Japanese, the Ministry of Construction has developed three affluence indices: household budget (per capita consumer expenditure); space dimensions (size of house, park areas, etc.); and time dimensions (work hours). In all three dimensions, individual Japanese lives were inferior to those of their counterparts in the United States and the United Kingdom. In fact, in none of these three indices does individual affluence in Japan exceed the affluence level of the national economy, and the time and space dimensions fall particularly far behind. In contrast, the standards of living in the United States and the United Kingdom are superior to their relative national economic power in all three dimensions.

Another measure of affluence is the so-called life GNP index, which includes both work hours and domestic purchasing power. According to the *White Paper on Construction*, Japanese per capita GNP is more than 15 percent higher than American per capita GNP. In terms of actual working hours, however, it is only about 1.5 percent higher. When GNP is recalculated on the basis of the yen's actual purchasing power in Japan, it becomes only 64.52 percent of the American GNP. In other words, the actual yearly income of the average Japanese is less than two thirds that of the average American.[28]

EXTERNAL-MATERIAL VERSUS INTERNAL-SPIRITUAL AFFLUENCE

The duality of lifestyles in Japan—namely external-material affluence versus the pursuit of internal-spiritual satisfaction—contributes to the Japanese people's sense that something is missing in their lives. In their eagerness to duplicate the modern lifestyles of the West, Japanese may have misinterpreted the true meaning of an affluent society. Although Japanese young people seem to be more open to modern ideas, for the most part, they, too, are taken with the pursuit of empty materialism. According to the 1993 *White Paper on Leisure* prepared by the Leisure Development Center, the five most popular leisure activities in 1992 were dining out on special occasions, domestic travel, driving, karaoke, and frequenting bars or pubs.

But, interestingly enough, more Japanese today value spiritual affluence or personal fulfillment (57.4 percent) over material affluence (29.0 percent). Changes over the years since 1972 reveal that the number of people who consider spiritual affluence more important has been on the rise since 1980, and a higher proportion of these are women (60.5 percent) rather than men (53.9 percent).[29] Similarly, on the issue of *yutori* (or leisure-mindedness), while the majority of Japanese people (61.5 percent) feel they possess this quality, such sentiments are stronger among women (63.3 percent) than among men (59.3 percent). These trends suggest that as Japan moves toward the national goal of spiritual rather than material affluence, women are most likely to be leading the way.[30]

ALLEVIATING PROBLEMS OF LIFESTYLES

American government officials have recently attempted, namely through the Structural Impediments Initiative, to force Japan to truly internationalize not only its economic and business practices but also its social structure and lifestyle. Americans living in Japan have pointed out the following lifestyle impediments:[31]

Housing. Rental fees, including deposit, gratuity, real estate agent costs, and advance rent, are exorbitant; Japanese landlords prefer not to rent to foreigners, families with children, and the elderly.

Shopping. Large-scale stores close too early; wrappings of produce and others are excessive.

Banking. Services are not available in the evenings or on holidays; handling fees for money transfers are expensive.

Telecommunications. Telephone installation is too expensive; specifications regarding long-distance calls are not made clear by the telephone company.

Transportation. Services end too early at night; train and subway companies operate on different fare scales; airfare is too expensive; highway tolls are too expensive; taxi drivers refuse to serve foreign and/or female customers.

Employment. Sex, age, and racial discrimination occur in the recruitment process; employees' activities are controlled to a great extent by the employing organization even during off-duty hours.

Hospitals. Patients are given no privacy; making appointments is not commonly practiced; very little explanation is provided about one's illnesses or medications.

Education. Educational programs for foreign children and returnee Japanese have not been properly established.

Restaurants. Bills are not always clearly specified; tables for nonsmokers are insufficient.

Local administration. New residents face a complexity of registration requirements; alien registration is too complicated.

Environment. Noise pollution is extreme in all public places; recreational facilities such as parks and museums close too early.

Most Japanese people would agree that, in all of these respects, the systems in Japan are irrational and inconvenient. But because they have become accustomed to this lifestyle, Japanese do not complain. They accept the national life structure and lifestyle as the core of their culture and realize that change, even if necessary for greater integration with other nations of the world, will be a slow and arduous process.

NOTES

1. Daini Den Den, 1993.

2. Prime Minister's Office, 1993c, 39–45.

3. See, for example, Amaya, 1990; Economic Planning Agency, 1989; 1990; Esaka and Kusaka, 1990; Fujioka, 1989; Ministry of Construction, 1990; Ministry of Labor, 1990; Prime Minister's Office, 1990d, 1990e, 1990f; Shitamori, 1989; Takada, 1989; Y. Takeuchi, 1990.

4. Although objective measurements of quality of life are difficult to ascertain, substantial progress has been made in measuring people's sense of well-being and in determining the important interrelationships among various aspects of the quality of life. Much of the empirical work on life quality in the 1960s and early 1970s focused on finding effective ways to measure well-being and applying those measures to the general population (Gurin, Veroff, and Feld, 1960; Bradburn, 1969; Andrews and Withey, 1976; Campbell, Converse, and Rodgers, 1976). Campbell et al. (1976) and A. Campbell (1980) are the benchmark studies for conceptualizing and measuring the psychological quality of American life.

Since then, three quite different approaches have been taken to define the life quality concept. The first approach rests on subjective analyses of life quality, oriented primarily toward individual psychological and demographic factors (Abbey and Andrews, 1985; Bryant and Veroff, 1984; Gilmartin, et al., 1979; Allardt, 1976; Andrews and Withey, 1976; Headey, 1981; Rabier, 1974; Shin, Kim, and Lee, 1982; Ortiz and Arce, 1986; Jackson, Chatters, and Neighbors, 1986; Bachman, Johnston, and O'Malley, 1986; Herzog and Rodgers, 1986). The second relies on structural analyses of life quality considered within the broader social context (House, 1980, 1981, 1986, 1987; House et al., 1979; Kessler, 1979; Kessler and Cleary, 1980; Kessler and Essex, 1982; Kessler and McRae, 1981; Alwin, Converse, and Martin, 1986; Thornton, Chang, and Sun, 1986; Sutton and Kahn, 1986), and the third adopts an interdisciplinary perspective by incorporating both social and psychological factors (Abbey, Dunkel-Schetter, and Brickman, 1983; Abbey and Andrews, 1985; Billings and Moos, 1981; Caplan, 1979; French, Rodgers and Cobb, 1974; Lazarus, 1981; Lavee, McCubbin, and Olson, 1987; Perlin and Schooler, 1978; Silver and Wortman, 1980; Weingarten and Bryant, 1987). Recently, attempts have been made to analyze well-being through interactions among social, psychological, and physiological environments (Lin and Ensel, 1989) and psychological, cultural, and structural factors (Kumagai, 1989a).

5. NSI is composed of three dimensions and 147 indicators: livelihood (eight fields, eighty-four indices), subjective attitudes (eleven indices), and interests (six fields, fifty-two indices). The eight fields of the livelihood dimension are economic stability, health, family life, working life, community and social activities, environment and safety, learning, and cultural activities. Yano-Kota Memorial Society, 1993, 502.

6. Economic Planning Agency, 1994b. In June 1993, a survey group of 5,000 Japanese men and women between the ages of fifteen and seventy-four years was randomly selected and asked to respond to the questionnaire; 4,192 people responded, a response rate of 82.8 percent.

7. Ibid., 20–21, figure 5–1.

8. Ibid., 22–25, figure 5–4.

9. Ibid., 56–59.

10. Prime Minister's Office, 1994c. This questionnaire survey has been conducted every year since 1969. In December 1993, 10,000 Japanese men and women over twenty years of age were selected for interviews throughout Japan, and the response rate was 70.8 percent.

11. Yano-Kota Memorial Society, 1993, 502.

12. Statistics Bureau, Management and Coordination Agency, 1993, *Kakei Chosa Hokoku*, reported in Yano-Kota Memorial Society, 1993, 499.

13. Statistics Bureau, Management and Coordination Agency, 1993, *Annual Report on the Family Income and Expenditure Survey*, reported in ibid., 502, table 48–6.

14. Economic Planning Agency, *Retail Price Report of 1991*, reported in Asahi, 1993, 199. Ten kilograms of rice in Tokyo cost ¥3,724 versus ¥1,882 in New York; 100 grams of beef in Tokyo cost ¥399 versus ¥143 yen in New York; and one kilogram of oranges in Tokyo cost ¥651 versus ¥375 in New York.

15. *Japan Economic Journal*, 1994a. A total of 1,403 students and salaried workers residing within thirty kilometers were interviewed in the fall of 1993. Valid responses were 820 (58.4 percent response rate).

16. As proof of succession, the emperor succeeds Three Sacred Treasures to the Imperial House.

17. Economic Planning Agency, *Household Consumer Report*, reported in Yano-Kota Memorial Society, 1993, 511.

18. Statistics Bureau of the Management and Coordination Agency, 1990, 1.

19. Ibid., 9; Asahi, 1993, 203; Yano-Kota Memorial Society, 1993, 508-510.

20. Ministry of Construction, *Construction Statistics*, 1990, reported in Yano-Kota Memorial Society, 1993: 510, table 48–13.

21. Ministry of Construction, *White Paper on Construction*, 1989, reported in ibid., table 48–14.

22. Economic Planning Agency, 1994a: 8–13.

23. Ibid., 6–8; Uehata, 1993.

24. Economic Planning Agency, 1994a, 7. Some 2,983 cases between June 1988 and June 1992. Ministry of Health and Welfare, 1990b.

25. Prime Minister's Office, 1994b, 2–3, table 1. In an effort to create a society of equal partnership between men and women, in October 1993 the Prime Minister's Office conducted interviews of Japanese people twenty years and older (2,124 respondents with a response rate of 70.8 percent).

26. Ibid., 4–5, table 2.

27. Prime Minister's Office, 1993c, 6–20.

28. Ministry of Construction, 1990, 8–9.

29. Prime Minister's Office, 1993c, 60–62.

30. Ibid., 36–38.

31. *Japan Economic Journal*, 1990f, 11

CHAPTER 3

Emerging Family Problems

As the internationalization of Japanese society progresses, new problems have begun to emerge. The dramatic increase in Japanese foreign direct investments, especially in the Southeast Asian region in the 1970s followed by the North American continent during the mid-1980s, means that more and more families are residing abroad, at least temporarily. This relocation process has resulted in intense stress on all family members, resulting in many important new problems for the Japanese family system.

JAPANESE MARRIAGE AND PARENTHOOD IN FOREIGN CULTURES

In October 1992, the total number of Japanese people residing abroad for more than three months was 425,000. Of these, approximately 3 out of 10 (124,000 and 29.1 percent) were minors, and about half were school-age children. Over the past decade, the total number of Japanese children attending schools abroad has increased by 43 percent, amounting to 50,842 in the spring of 1993.[1] Most of these children (41.8 percent) resided in North America, followed by 25.3 percent in Europe and 23.6 percent in Asia.

While the actual number of children living abroad has been increasing, the proportion of those children in elementary school has been declining continuously over the same ten-year period. At the same time, the number of children in the other three age groups, preschool, junior high school, and senior high school, has been on the rise, suggesting that Japanese overseas employees have come to comprise various age levels.

Prior to the recent wave of Japanese foreign direct investment, families assigned abroad were, in general, of high socioeconomic status. Considered members of the Japanese business elite, husbands were typically affiliated with governmental bureaus, trading companies, and financial firms, engaged in white-collar jobs rather than in product manufacturing. Recently, however, a sizable number of engineers and technicians have been assigned overseas to facilitate plant operation, to supervise product manufacturing, and to train local workers. Most of these workers never expected foreign assignments—and much less so their families. Therefore, they are not well prepared for foreign assignment or equipped with the skills necessary to adjust to foreign life.

Of the Japanese children living in North America, Europe, and Asia, 35.7 percent attended full-time Japanese schools, 40.9 percent studied both at Japanese Saturday schools and local schools concurrently, and 23.4 percent attended local schools only. Regional contrasts are evident. Namely, in developing countries such as Asia, South America, the Middle East, and Africa, the majority of Japanese children attend full-time Japanese schools. In Europe, however, approximately equal proportions of Japanese children receive education at each of the three alternative educational institutions. Finally, in North America, the majority of children (74.2 percent) attend Japanese Saturday schools and local schools concurrently, but very few study at full-time Japanese schools.

These different educational patterns are directly correlated to the number of Japanese schools in each region. Mainly because there are very few full-time Japanese schools in North America, only 3.7 percent of all the Japanese children in this region were able to attend them.[2] According to a 1993 report of the Ministry of Foreign Affairs, of the eighty-eight full-time Japanese schools around the world, only three are in North America: one in New York, one in Chicago, and one in Atlanta. In contrast, 75, or nearly half, of the 165 Japanese Saturday schools worldwide are in the United States and Canada.

PROBLEMS OF THE JAPANESE FAMILY ABROAD

Recent studies, including group discussion interviews and question-naires, have been conducted to uncover the problems encountered by Japanese families stationed overseas.[3] Japanese mothers (average age of thirty-seven years) with school-age children were selected for the study. Seven Japanese manufacturers in the American West, Midwest, and mid-South cooperated with this research project, administering questionnaires in Japanese during the spring of 1988.[4] Interview sessions were conducted with Japanese mothers, American teachers at a local academy, and Japanese directors and instructors at two Japanese Saturday schools in different southern U.S. cities. The total number of questionnaires completed was 146. These seven sites were then visited in the fall of 1988, and group discussion interviews were conducted with the Japanese mothers temporarily residing there. An additional set of interviews was conducted in the winter of 1994. At each site, approximately ten Japanese mothers whose husbands were affiliated with the cooperating Japanese companies participated in the group discussion. These two sets of studies reveal strikingly similar research results, despite their being more than five years apart.

In an effort to draw a composite picture of the problems that Japanese families living in the United States must face, the studies explored a number of factors, including family life and parenthood, life satisfaction, quality of life, family stresses and strains, social support, and gender roles. Although the historical backgrounds and operating conditions of the seven Japanese companies involved differed markedly, the voices of Japanese mothers across the two sets of studies and over a five-year span were strikingly similar. Some important generalizations about the problems of Japanese families abroad can be derived from their responses.

Japanese Mothers' Command of English

The ability of families to adjust to a foreign culture is enhanced by knowing the language. But most Japanese mothers expressed difficulty in conducting sophisticated conversations in English. Examples of situations in which communication problems frequently arose included explaining problems of electrical appliances over the phone, making airline ticket reservations over the phone, consulting with American medical doctors, and talking with schoolteachers. American ESL (English as a Second Language) teachers pointed out that Japanese mothers' extremely limited command of English often hinders their children's adjustment to American classrooms.

Perhaps due to this lack of language skills, the number of American friends with whom Japanese mothers feel at ease is extremely small. Approximately one third of the respondents had no American friends at all, another one third had only one, and one fifth had two. In contrast, these mothers make Japanese friends in America relatively easily.

Short-term Overseas Assignments

The average length of stay of a Japanese family in the United States is 3.3 years. This relatively short period of assignment only increases the problems Japanese families face in adjusting to American life. Not only does it limit opportunities to acquire English conversational skills, but Japanese children at American schools often find themselves treated as unwelcome visitors. Rarely composing more than one third of the student body in an American school, Japanese children tend to become easy targets for bullying by the other children.[5]

Nearly one third of the Japanese mothers interviewed identified their return to Japan as something they most look forward to in the near future, indicating a very low degree of adjustment to American life and the likelihood that they are not making the most out of their families' experience living abroad. Their principal concerns while living in America are children's education (47.2 percent), poor command of English (15 percent), children's education upon return to Japan (10.2 percent), and health of the family members (9.4 percent).

The relatively short period of their overseas assignments also lessens the sense of involvement of Japanese families in community life. In fact, of the 146 Japanese mothers who responded to the questionnaire in 1988, only 2 participated in volunteer activities. This tendency toward minimal community involvement among Japanese mothers in American communities has not improved to any noticeable extent even today. According to the director of a Japanese Saturday school who also acts as counselor to the Japanese families, most mothers tend to develop an extremely narrow social interaction network composed of 20 to 80 Japanese wives and intended primarily for the exchange of gossip.[6]

It is in this regard that Americans are most critical of Japanese living in their communities, expecting parents to be more involved in community activities since their children are reaping the benefits of attending American public schools. American teachers in particular regret the low level of involvement of Japanese parents in school and community activities, including the local PTA meetings. Since these gatherings usually take place in the evening, Japanese mothers, who are uneasy about their English-language capabilities in the first place, would prefer to stay home in order to greet their husbands when they return from work.[7]

Dependency on Husbands

Japanese wives in America are highly dependent on their husbands: 30.6 percent agreed strongly with the statement "I would feel completely lost if I didn't have my husband," and 43.1 percent agreed somewhat. But most mothers still assume the major responsibility for their children's socialization in the community (66.2 percent versus only 7.4 percent of fathers).

Interestingly enough, it is in this area that many husbands and wives disagree. Arguments about children's education and children's socialization were cited by 20.8 percent and 14.6 percent of the mothers, respectively. These results may reflect the fact that the power of Japanese mothers has been traditionally confined to the domestic arena. Unfortunately, the inability of Japanese mothers to serve as power figures outside the home can have a detrimental effect on the cross-cultural adjustment of their children, leaving them with feelings of insecurity in their peer relationships with American children.

Family Stresses and Strains

Responses of Japanese mothers living in the United States further reveal that life overseas is highly stressful for both parents and children: increasing difficulties in managing children, 48.5 percent; increasing strain on family money for medical expenses, clothes, food, education, home care, and so on, 32.4 percent; increase in sibling rivalry, 30.4 percent; and increase in arguments between parents and children, 28.8 percent.

Although Japanese mothers want to discuss their children's problems with the teachers at school, their poor command of English prevents them from doing so. And since fathers work until late in the evening (6.3 percent of the mothers identified this as their most serious conjugal problem), mothers have no one to turn to.

In times of real crisis, Japanese residing in the United States have been unable to receive the professional assistance they require. Hampered by poor English skills, Japanese mothers are reluctant to seek help from American counselors, a growing number of whom resent the fact that these mothers cannot speak English. Japanese businessmen also suffer. In some cases, husbands of *tanshin funin* (unaccompanied by their families) have suffered serious nervous breakdowns, forcing them to return to Japan in less than a year.[8] Clearly, there is an acute need for Japanese counselors to assist Japanese families trying to make their way abroad.

Children's Education

Japanese mothers' expectations for their children's educational achievement are extremely high. The great majority (71 percent) consider it important for their children to successfully advance to higher educational institutions, and 26.5 percent consider it very important.

These attitudes are reflected in their children's activities. Japanese children in the United States must cope with an extremely heavy study load: local school education, ESL program, Japanese Saturday school education, correspondence courses on Japanese subjects, and private lessons in music, arts, or sports. Additional studies are viewed as necessary for keeping up with the Japanese curriculum. Otherwise, these children will face serious problems in meeting the strictly standardized requirements of the Japanese curriculum upon their return home. Japanese Saturday school education, considered essential to the socialization of Japanese children living abroad, is obviously insufficient for reviewing the standard one-week Japanese school curriculum.[9]

Children spend almost equal time on homework (2.6 hours on weekdays, 1.3 hours on Saturday, and 1.8 hours on Sunday) and playing with other children (2.5 hours on weekdays, 2.2 hours on Saturday, and 2.1 hours on Sunday). In many cases, Japanese children play with their Japanese peers rather than other American children, and they continue to communicate in Japanese. They also spend relatively long hours watching television (2.2 hours on weekdays, 2.7 hours on Saturday, and 3 hours on Sunday), perhaps indicative of their relative isolation at school and in the community.

Due to the recent influx of Japanese families in the United States, Japanese children sometimes consider it nonessential to acquire English-language skills as a means of communicating at school or in the community. In fact, one respondent reported that Japanese students numbered 200 in one southern California high school of 1,200 students. And in many New York City schools, Japanese students amount to one third of the total student body.[10] Japanese mothers have relatively favorable opinions of local school programs, particularly with regard to their ability to respond to individual needs: 78.4 percent reported that they are fair and 10.8 percent good; curricula are reported as just about right by 75.7 percent. Several subjects, however, are found in need of improvement: ESL, 46.4 percent; mathematics, 17.9 percent; music, 10.7 percent; and physical education, 7.1 percent. ESL programs, specifically intended to assist long-term immigrants in acquiring English-language skills, are not really geared to Japanese children whose stay in the United States is temporary. In this sense, Japanese families should be willing to allocate appropriate means and facilities if they want these programs strengthened.

Satisfaction of Japanese Mothers

Japanese mothers' levels of satisfaction were examined in terms of their roles as mother, homemaker, and wife, and in all measures, high levels of satisfaction emerged. More than 8 out of every 10 of the mothers interviewed expressed their enjoyment of motherhood; approximately 9 out of 10 were satisfied with their homemaker roles; and even more were happy being married. Of the 146 Japanese mothers interviewed in 1988, only 5 (3.4 percent) worked outside the home, and of the 20 housewives with children who were interviewed in 1994, none worked outside the home.

CARE FOR THE ELDERLY PARENTS LEFT IN JAPAN

The advanced rate of aging of Japanese society, combined with the continued preference for coresidency living arrangements among the elderly, poses serious problems for Japanese families living abroad. In most cases, relocating elderly parents to foreign countries is unrealistic. So when independent living for the elderly is impossible, alternative family caretakers nonexistent, and public institutionalization unacceptable, there are no ready solutions for the Japanese family sent overseas. Effective measures for coping with this important aspect of overseas life have yet to be proposed.

THE TRADITIONAL FAMILY IN A MODERN ERA

The coexistence of tradition and modernity within the Japanese family compounds all of the hardships faced by Japanese families living abroad: Cross-cultural experiences are viewed as detrimental to children's socialization; women confine themselves to traditional sex roles of homemaker and motherhood; the interdependency of mother-child ties is intensified; and responsibilities for elderly parents are all-consuming.

This is not to say that traditional family values in Japan are without inherent virtue. But real problems arise when this dual pattern of tradition and modernity must, in accordance with the forces of internationalization, be transplanted in foreign and more authentically "modern" cultures. "When in Rome, do as the Romans do" is a prescription much easier followed when the roots of tradition do not bind thought and action as they do within the Japanese family.

AMERICAN ATTITUDES TOWARD JAPANESE COMMUNITIES IN THE UNITED STATES

With the collapse of the Japanese bubble economy in the summer of 1991, American attitudes toward Japanese residing in their communities have shown a change for the worse.

During the course of the interviews conducted in the winter of 1994, the increasingly negative sentiments of Americans were referred to repeatedly by Japanese businessmen and counselors. These sentiments are in marked contrast to the more positive attitudes elicited from Americans during the latter half of the 1980s and into the 1990s when the Japanese economy was in full bloom and Japanese direct investments in the United States were extremely successful. Perhaps as a result of the gradual recovery of the U.S. economy, Americans are no longer intimidated by the Japanese, and expressions of animosity and negativism are more in vogue.

Numerous factors contribute to and/or reflect this increasing American hostility: Americans laid off by Japanese-owned companies have sued these companies since they assumed that layoffs would never occur even under the worst economic circumstances; American workers have become increasingly anxious about losing their jobs; an increasing number of local American newspapers run negative articles about Japan; more American opinion leaders have begun to voice negative opinions about Japan; enrollments in Japanese language courses at American community colleges and universities are on the decline; and expenditures for the education of Japanese children at public schools have increased the American tax burden. The Japanese community must be sensitive to this burgeoning negativism in local American communities, and public sector intervention is most definitely required to offset these unwanted frictions.

SOCIAL POLICIES RELATING TO JAPANESE FAMILIES ABROAD

If Japan's incorporation within the international community is to be complete, joint efforts must be made by business and government leaders to establish comprehensive support programs for Japanese families living abroad, especially with regard to the education of children. The nature of the problem is complicated and extends beyond any single jurisdiction. Therefore, various ministries in Japan must cooperate with each other, even though they are notoriously known for their administrative sectionalism. It is encouraging to note, however, that changes are currently under way to reorganize central government ministries and agencies so that they represent more comprehensive and cohesive units. The creation of a new Japanese Ministry of People's Life, which will combine functions of the Ministry of Health and Welfare and the Ministry of Labor, is indicative of this trend.[11]

Nevertheless, the Japanese practice of entrusting social welfare to the private sector is clearly remiss in addressing the problems of overseas families and of the elderly parents left in Japan. Without recourse to public support, these family members have been forced to look inward for solutions.

Clearly, the most serious problem that overseas families face is the education of their children. In Japan, full-time schools and Japanese Saturday schools are organized and subsidized by the Ministry of Education. Despite the fact that primary school education is compulsory in Japan, educating children at Japanese full-time schools or Saturday schools overseas is not free; these schools are considered supplemental to local school education.[12] And although the majority of Japanese today receive a high school education, there is no government-supported overseas Japanese high school.

The lack of governmental support for overseas Saturday schools is evidenced in the extremely low financial assistance (in one case, $504 per month in 1988, raised to $621 per month in the 1993-1994 academic year) given these institutions. Since only the principals of the schools are sent by the Japanese government, the rest of the schools' personnel must be recruited and financed locally, and operating expenses can be quite high.

Overseas Japanese schools confront a host of other problems. Recruiting local instructors with appropriate teachers' certificates and teaching experience for Japanese school programs is extremely difficult. Candidates tend to be Japanese graduate students on American campuses or Japanese housewives residing in the area. School authorities cannot expect long-term commitments from these temporary instructors.

Appropriate levels of Japanese-language instruction are also difficult to determine since some children still use Japanese as their primary means of communication, while others, born or raised in the United States, rely heavily on English.

Finally, Japanese mothers tend to demand too much from overseas Saturday schools. Rather than recognizing the supplementary nature of this instruction, they often expect Saturday schools to cover in five hours all of the weekly assignments that their children would receive if they were attending school in Japan. In order to facilitate the smooth transition of families overseas, the Ministry of Education must reevaluate its overall management of overseas Japanese schools.

NOTES

1. Ministry of Foreign Affairs, 1992, reported in Japan Overseas Educational Services, 1993, 7; *Japan Economic Journal*, 1994e.

2. Japan Overseas Educational Services, 1993, 7.

3. Kumagai, 1988a, 1988c, 1989a, 1989b, 1989c, 1989d, 1990a, 1990c.

4. Another objective of this project was to analyze American employees' attitudes toward working for U.S.-based Japanese companies. Various cross-cultural problems are identified in the study. Therefore, in order to preserve the anonymity of these Japanese manufacturers, it was agreed that any information that might identify their corporate names not be disclosed.

5. Cunningham, 1988, 130–144.

6. Personal interview conducted with a director of a Japanese Saturday school in Kentucky, January 19, 1994.

7. Group interviews with American teachers at a private academy in Alabama, January 24, 1994.

8. Personal interview conducted with a director of a Japanese Saturday school in Kentucky, January 19, 1994.

9. Discussion with Japanese instructors at a Japanese Saturday school in Alabama, January 22, 1994.

10. Craft, 1991; *Japan Economic Journal*, 1993g.

11. Reported in *Japan Economic Journal*, 1994d.

12. Although fees to be born by Japanese parents to educate their children in Japanese Saturday schools vary across institutions, for the 1993–1994 academic year in Alabama the fee was U.S.$300 for one year, or U.S.$100 per term.

PART II

EDUCATION AND YOUTH

CHAPTER 4

The Japanese Educational System

The importance of traditional family values in Japanese life extends to the unique nature of the modern Japanese education system. The first step in understanding this essential interplay of family and education is to examine the historical development of the Japanese education system itself.[1]

DEVELOPMENT OF THE EDUCATIONAL SYSTEM

Since as early as the first half of the nineteenth century, when Japan was still in the feudal age, Japanese people placed a high value on education. At that time, the samurai (or warlord) class was in charge of political affairs. They established schools within their feudal domains to teach samurai children the moral values, cultural appreciation, and martial arts necessary for carrying out their future duties. There were also 20,000 *terakoya* (literally, temple schools, though they were not generally run by temples) operating throughout the country to teach reading, writing, and arithmetic to the children of farmers and townsfolk who needed such skills in their daily life. Attendance at temple schools was on a purely voluntary basis; there was no system of compulsory education. About 40 percent of the children of farmers and townsfolk are estimated to have studied at such schools.

In 1872, when Japan first began to modernize, the newly formed Meiji government established a compulsory system of integrated Western-style education. Extending from elementary school to university, this system was intended to foster the development of industry and culture throughout Japan. The government stated: "We look forward to a time when there will be no illiteracy in any village house, no illiterate in any home."

In 1900, as many as 90 percent of Japanese children six years and older were attending school for the compulsory four years. By 1907, the school term was increased to six years, and the proportion of children in school reached 99 percent. In subsequent years, numerous elementary schools, middle schools, high schools, girls' high schools, vocational schools, colleges, and universities were founded. For all except elementary schools, applicants had to be selected for entrance; so the number of students continuing on to higher levels of education remained low. The percentage of elementary school students going on to secondary school in 1935 was just 18.5 percent, and only 3 percent went on to receive higher education. Not until 1947 was compulsory education extended to nine years.

THE JAPANESE EDUCATIONAL SYSTEM TODAY

Three outstanding characteristics define the educational system in contemporary Japan: standardization, dual structure, and shared responsibilities.

The Standardized System

The modern Japanese educational system is composed of six years of elementary school, three years of junior high school, three years of senior high school, and four years of university. The first nine years of instruction in elementary and junior high school are compulsory. This standardized system of national education was established in 1947 under the directorship of the U.S. occupation forces after World War II. Primary and secondary school curricula are established by the Ministry of Education, and all materials for classroom use must be authorized by the

Figure 4–1
Japanese School System

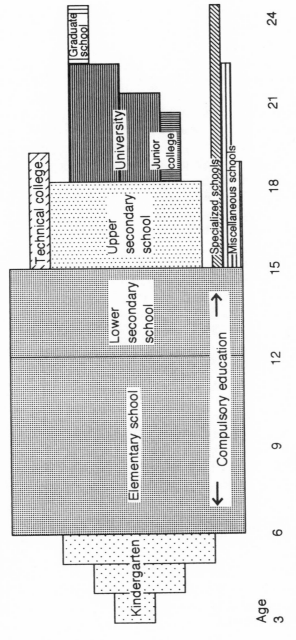

Source: Asahi Shimbun, 1993, 238.

ministry. Thus, contrary to the U.S. system of state government administration, education in Japan stems directly from the federal authorities.

In 1993 the proportions of students continuing on to senior high school and higher educational institutions were 96.2 (males: 95.3 percent; females: 97.2 percent) and 34.5 percent (males: 26.6 percent; females: 42.4 percent), respectively.[2] Although the senior high school curriculum is not formally a part of compulsory education, the majority of Japanese people today consider it necessary. Hence, the proportion of students advancing to high school is remarkably high.

The heart of the Japanese educational system is its emphasis on standardized instruction, rather than the development of students' creativity. Recent efforts to modify this system have met with little success. Although a few "unique" entrance examinations have been designed to award creativity over rote answers, students studying for these exams and schools administering them still prepared model test answers that the students were taught to memorize. In Japan's meritocratic society, the content of education is valued less than the prestige of graduating from one of the nation's top schools.

Given the recent decline in the population of children under fifteen years of age (16.7 percent of the total Japanese population),[3] the number of educational institutions has declined sharply over the years. In 1993, the total number of elementary schools in Japan attended by children between six and twelve years of age was 24,676 (1955: 26,883), and that of junior high schools attended by children between thirteen and fifteen years of age was 11,292 (1955: 13,767). Although the total number of high schools has remained fairly constant since 1990, a future decline can be expected. The total number of secondary educational institutions in Japan were 4,607 in 1955, 5,453 in 1985, 5,506 in 1990, and 5,501 in 1993.[4]

Attrition in the children's population has also affected the increasing trend toward no class on Saturday. From the start of Japan's formal education system in the Meiji period, it has been the principle of school authorities to keep children at school six days a week, including a half day on Saturday. However, with the increasing popularity of a five-day workweek (Monday through Friday) in Japan, more parents are finding it inconvenient for their children to attend school on Saturday mornings. Therefore, in September 1992, the Ministry of Education declared that the second Saturday of every month would be a nonschool day at public educational institutions.

Although this new system has been regarded as an epoch-making educational revolution, it has not been made mandatory for Japan's private educational institutions, and many have refused to adopt it. Free from government supervision of their curriculum administration and faced with tremendous pressure to adequately prepare their students for the rigorous entrance examination system, many private schools continue to follow their own programs of education. Of all the private educational institutions in Japan in 1993, more than half of the senior high schools (51.1 percent of 1,301), elementary schools (63.6 percent of 165), and kindergartens (87.0 percent of 8,552) now follow the one-Saturday-off-per-month system, but only one-third of the junior high schools (32.6 percent of 559) do. Low rates are especially pronounced in urban regions such as Tokyo (17.0 percent), Osaka (11.8 percent), and Fukuoka (9.1 percent).[5]

In an effort to increase the leisure time enjoyed by children, the Ministry of Education plans to extend the no-class-on-Saturday system from one to two days per month beginning in the 1995–1996 academic year. However, it is not certain that Japanese parents truly appreciate their children's need to enjoy time off from school. Given the extraordinary amount of pressure placed on students to excel in a rigorous educational system, it is possible that informal instruction at Saturday schools will replace the mandatory classroom hours.

The Dual Structure

Accepted modes of upward social mobility have been identified as crucial in shaping a nation's school system. Some researchers have contrasted the English norm of sponsored mobility with the American norm of contest mobility.[6] Under English norms, the existing elite grant elite status to those not born to it but nevertheless deserving it. Under American norms, elite status is thought to be the prize of an open contest. It is argued that these varied norms account for the divergence between the English and American systems of social control and education.

The dual structure of the Japanese educational system combines British elements of sponsored mobility and American elements of contest mobility. Under the fierce "examination hell" system, Japanese children are pressured to pass rigorous examinations from the early years of their education through to entrance into colleges and universities. This phase of education in Japan clearly fits the contest mobility norms of upward social mobility. At each level, the amount of information the students can retain is more important than any creative ability they might demonstrate, so long hours of study are essential.

Once a student crosses the rigorous hurdle of the college entrance examination, however, the system becomes one of sponsored mobility. Pressures are removed from Japanese college students, and only a tiny fraction regard college as a place to study and learn. Thus, most of the one third of Japanese high school graduates who advance to higher education fill their college days with a wide range of social and other activities—the so-called "leisure-land syndrome."[7]

This dual structure of contest and sponsored mobility is one of the most important factors setting the Japanese educational system apart from its Western counterparts—and perhaps one of the greatest structural impediments for the internationalization of Japanese society.

Shared Responsibilities

Another integral component of Japanese education is its system of shared responsibilities between teacher and student, mother and child, and formal and informal curricula.

Mastery of examination skills is the shared responsibility of the teacher and student. The teacher's emphasis on quantity of information over analytical or creative ability is respected by students. Indeed, the entire reputation of the teacher is based on the number of students who move on to respectable institutions.

Examination hell is faced by mother and child together. The mother's responsibility is to create an ideal study environment for her child. She devotes herself to caring for her beloved child by serving snacks late in the evening and even accompanying her child to the college entrance examination. A typical Japanese mother protects and cares for her children like a lioness protects her cubs, and the father is likely to know little, if anything, of his children's personal lives. With very little free time, few opportunities to socialize, and very protective parents, it is very difficult for Japanese children to become socially adept, and many lack the requisite skills for interacting amicably with their playmates.[8]

Another example of shared responsibility in Japanese education is the *juku* (or cram school) system. On top of their formal schooling, a large number of Japanese students attend after-hours cram school in order to acquire better skills for passing the entrance examination. Education-minded mothers (or *kyoiku-mama*) spend a lot of time searching for prestigious cram schools that have high rates of students passing the entrance examinations of good schools.

Providing Japanese children with ideal educational environments is a costly undertaking, and it imposes a heavy financial burden on the family. According to a 1993 report by the Ministry of Education, the average costs for a public school education in 1991–92 were ¥201,511 ($2,000) for kindergarten, ¥230,094 ($2,300) for elementary school, ¥275,195 ($2,750) for junior high school, and ¥352,188 ($3,500) for senior high school.[9] Costs for after-hours instruction, in the form of cram schools, special tutors, and private lessons, accounted for a significant portion of these expenses: 59.3 percent for a child in elementary school; 48.6 percent for a junior high school student, and 13.9 percent for a senior high school student. It is interesting to note that the cost for junior high school students exceeds that of senior high school students. Attending a good senior high school is considered imperative for successfully advancing to a prestigious higher educational institution in Japan. Therefore, Japanese parents must spend more money for their children's junior high school education.

With the attrition in the children's population, competition for survival among cram schools has intensified. Although there are no exact figures, it is estimated that there are approximately 40,000 to 50,000 *juku* throughout Japan.[10] Education-minded mothers are eager to place their children in the best of these schools, hoping this will lead their beloved children down the golden path of educational success.

INTERDEPENDENCY BETWEEN THE FAMILY AND EDUCATION

The interdependency between the family and educational institutions in Japan, combined with the internationalization of Japanese society, has resulted in a number of interesting social phenomena, namely education-minded mothers as discussed above, *tanshin funin* (business bachelors), and TCKs (Third Culture Kids, or *kikokushijo* in Japanese). These phenomena indicate that the structure of the Japanese family and interfamily relations is evolving to accommodate the needs of the children's education.

Tanshin funin describes the situation where a married man is transferred to another job, but his family remains behind so that the children's schooling can continue uninterrupted. These men are forced to lead a bachelor's life mainly for the sake of their children's education. Today more than one third of the total number of married transferred employees are *tanshin funin*, and the rate rises with the age of the employee. Rates for those in their early forties, late forties, and over fifty were 40 percent, 52.9 percent, and 53.7 percent, respectively.[11]

Third Culture Kids are those who are partly raised and educated abroad because of their parents' foreign assignments. The product of diverse educational and social influences, these children often face difficulties in readjusting to Japanese society and particularly the standardized system of Japanese education.

The number of returnee children enrolled in Japanese schools has doubled in the ten years between 1976 and 1985,[12] and some higher institutions have even begun to set quotas for returnee children's admission, administering separate entrance examinations to them. Although their readjustment to Japanese life is directly related to the age they left and returned to Japan,[13] most of these students experience a shared sense of "differentness" when they return to school in Japan. Common readjustment problems include language, study habits, curriculum requirements, rules and regulations, peer relationships, manners, and customs.[14]

Problems experienced by returnee children reflect the nature of the Japanese educational system as well as some of the more fundamental aspects of Japanese society as a whole. Returnee children are pressured to adjust to a rigid Japanese social system that fails to appreciate their cross-cultural experiences and their internationally minded personalities. But it is precisely these children who will ultimately take the lead in forging Japan's future path toward intercultural communication and true international understanding.

IMPACT OF CROSS-CULTURAL EDUCATION

The internationalization of Japan is destined to impact the educational system in two primary ways. First, Japanese children living and studying abroad will bring back to the home country new attitudes, values, knowledge, and skills. Second, foreign students living and studying in Japan will influence the teachers, students, and families with whom they come in contact.

Trends in Foreign Study of Japanese

Until recently, *ryugaku* (or study abroad) usually referred to formal enrollment in a graduate or professional school or the engagement in research activities at higher educational institutions in foreign countries. Today, however, new types of foreign study have emerged.

Some Japanese, for example, study abroad with the avowed intention of acquiring the requisite language skills for enrolling in local universities and colleges. In many cases, however, they are more interested in the overall foreign experience than any educational training they might receive.

Other students receive a liberal arts education at a branch campus of an American university in Japan and then move on to their major curriculum of study at that university's main campus in the United States. Approximately sixty universities and colleges from various parts of the United States currently plan to open branch campuses in Japan.[14] These branch institutions have the potential for serving as important training grounds for internationally minded personnel and for counteracting the leisure-land syndrome that pervades most Japanese college campuses. Japanese students trained in these cross-cultural environments are bound to develop more independent attitudes and a greater sense of the importance of active participation in the education process.

Still other Japanese students are formally enrolled in American colleges or junior colleges after successfully passing interviews in Japan. This type of foreign study is more popular among female than male students, perhaps due to the limited job opportunities in Japan for those who obtain their higher education overseas. It is interesting to note, too, that some of the applicants for this type of foreign study are Japanese housewives, who make use of their experiences abroad by improving family interaction, child socialization, and community activism once they return to Japan.

The increased numbers and types of Japanese who are studying abroad is certain to have some impact on Japan's social value structure. But the extent of this impact remains unclear. Indeed, one longitudinal study of the effects of cross-cultural education on the attitudes and personalities of Japanese male graduate students revealed an increased appreciation for American society and culture, but not at the expense of a lowered appreciation for their own society and culture.[16] These findings parallel Japan's modernization process in the sense that adaptation to new cultures has never resulted in a loss of appreciation for traditional Japanese values and mores.

Foreign Students in Japan

The number of foreign students studying in Japan has been increasing steadily, as much as 900 percent between 1978 (5,849) and 1993 (52,405) (see Figure 4–2). Most of these students (91.6 percent) are from Asian countries; of them, 80 percent are from three countries, namely, China (42.1 percent), Korea (23.9 percent), and Taiwan (12.6 percent). Of the remaining, 2.5 percent, 2.2 percent and 1.6 percent are from North America, Europe, and Latin America, respectively.[17] By the beginning of the twenty-first century, the Ministry of Education aims to increase the number of foreign students in Japan to approximately 100,000, a number equivalent to that of Western nations and representing a virtual doubling of today's standing.

Foreign students in Japan must cope with numerous problems: Language is one of the most serious (38.3 percent), followed by financial problems (32.9 percent), differences in lifestyles and values (23.7 percent), having no friends (8.6 percent), and housing problems (8.5 percent).[18] Due to the high cost of living in Japan, foreign students who are not fortunate enough to find home hospitality with Japanese families must bear a tremendous housing burden. Of the total foreign students studying in Japan, nearly eight out of ten (77.5 percent) rent private rooms or apartments, and 40 percent of the students who reside in these private accommodations complain about the high rent and narrow space. With the support of a major economic organization in Tokyo, some Japanese corporations have begun to make their employees' dormitory facilities available to foreign students in need of housing. These arrangements may not only alleviate the housing problems faced by foreign students but afford them the opportunity to communicate with the Japanese employees who are living there.[19]

As the number of foreign students in Japan continues to increase, it is likely that more and more Japanese families will open their doors to these visitors on a home-stay basis. Not only are foreign students in such programs able to learn about Japanese culture and lifestyle, but the Japanese families themselves acquire a firsthand knowledge of foreign culture and values. These everyday interactions will serve to facilitate intercultural communication and to enhance international understanding.

Figure 4-2

Changes in the Number of Foreign Students Studying at Japanese Higher Educational Institutions by Type of Funds: 1978–1993

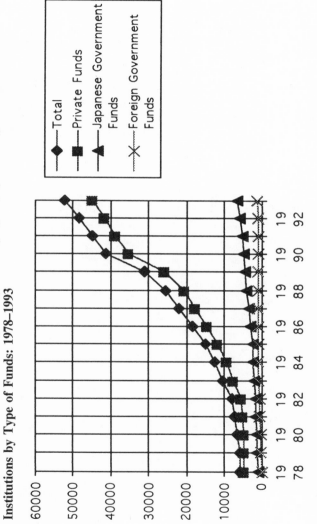

Source: Ministry of Education, 1994b, 2.

NOTES

1. The author's book *Kokusaika Shakai no Katei Kyoiku* (Japanese Family Education in the Era of International Society) examines this interplay between family and education in contemporary Japan (Kumagai, 1988c). This historical review of the Japanese education system draws heavily upon Nippon Steel Human Resources Development Co., 1988, 164–177; and Yano Kota Memorial Society, 1986, 473–476.

2. Ministry of Education, 1993a, 6, tables 9 and 10.

3. Management and Coordination Agency, 1994. Changes in the proportion of this age bracket are as follows: 31.62 percent in 1884; 36.68 percent in 1940; 30.04 percent in 1960; 21.51 percent in 1985; and 18.19 percent in 1990.

4. Ministry of Education, 1993a, tables 1–3.

5. Ministry of Education, 1993c.

6. Turner, 1960.

7. U.S. Department of Education, 1987; Kumagai, 1988a.

8. *Japan Economic Journal*, 1993f.

9. Ministry of Education, 1993b, 1, table 1.

10. *Japan Economic Journal,* 1994b.

11. Institute of Labor Administration, 1986, 7–8; Kumagai, 1988b, 127–136.

12. 1976: 4,598; 1982: 9,563; 1985: 10,196. Ministry of Education, 1986.

13. Nakatsu, 1989.

14. Ministry of Education, 1986, 74.

15. Kuroha, 1988.

16. Kumagai, 1988c.

17. Ministry of Education, 1994b, 3–4.

18. JETRO, 1989, 151; *Japan Economic Journal*, 1994c.

19. *Japan Economic Journal*, 1994c.

CHAPTER 5

Japanese Youth Today

Today approximately one in every seven people in Japan is an adolescent, roughly defined as someone between junior high school age and their early twenties.[1] A Japanese youth, therefore, is either a high school student, a college student, or a young worker.

SHINJINRUI

The Japanese younger generation is frequently called *shinjinrui*, meaning the new breed. Born in the 1960s or later, these Japanese youth share a number of interesting characteristics: Raised in an affluent society, they have no experience of poverty or starvation; they are whimsical, emotional, and playful; they display a cold reserve toward things that do not interest them; and they have extremely strong ties with peers.[2] A more critical analysis of this generation includes lack of commitment, indifference to larger issues, and unwillingness to grow up.[3]

Many of these characteristics can be attributed to the nature of Japanese society in which *shinjinrui* were raised. Born during postwar Japan's high economic growth period, this generation became of age in an era of rampant consumerism, increased leisure time, and vigorous pursuit of pleasure. Traditional lifestyles, values, and hierarchical orientations were fast disappearing. Thus, *shinjinrui* fell victim to Japan's uneven structural transformation: fast-paced materialistic advancement absent of any deep-rooted intellectual or spiritual fulfillment. For many, participation in such new religious sects as Omukyo and Moonies aids in their search for self-affirmation.[4]

Studies of the values and lifestyles of Japan's *dankai* juniors, or young people born mostly to the parents of the *dankai no sedai* (baby boomers born between 1946 and 1949) generation, reveal that their popular practice of dancing to radio cassette music in the Harajuku area of Tokyo is a means of expressing their originality. Through these performances they try to capture the attention of passersby. Many of these young people also participate in live bands that perform in the pedestrian malls of Harajuku and Shibuya.

These self-absorbed, rootless young people are struggling to find their place in Japan's pressure-filled, culturally controlled society. It is not surprising that many Japanese youths have difficulty settling into responsible adult roles. In fact, a growing number have fallen victim to what has become popularly known as the "Peter Pan syndrome"—extending the duration of their student lives, taking on temporary rather than permanent employment, or just doing nothing at all.

JAPAN'S COMIC BOOK CULTURE

Comic books (or *manga*) form the core of the Japanese youth culture, offering exciting, real-life dramas to stimulate their searching minds. These graphically powerful, determinedly escapist, and immensely enjoyable books, sometimes considered more popular than even television, have carefully developed plots that reduce even the most serious economic or political issues to everyday emotional scenarios with which Japanese youth can easily identify.[5]

Manga share several outstanding features that tend to attract young Japanese readers. First, they use large visual signs and symbols that make the meaning of the story clear to the readers. Second, they rely heavily on onomatopeia to express feelings in words that sound like that feeling. A headache, for example, can range from *chiku-chiku* (slight) to *gan-gan* (sledgehammer). Third, *manga* characters look strikingly Western, allowing the reader to maintain a psychological distance even though the characters are acting out their most cherished fantasies. Fourth, most *manga* are easy to read because they use the Japanese *hiragana* alphabet to spell out the pronunciation of kanji. And fifth, while their themes may not always be humorous, they realize the unattainable and make even the commonplace seem interesting.

The wide circulation of even a single *manga* is evidence of the integral role these publications play in popular Japanese culture. Of the numerous *manga* magazines currently published, a tremendously popular one entitled *Shukan Shonen Jampu* (or Jump as it is popularly called) just celebrated its twenty-fifth anniversary in the summer of 1993. *Jump's* success derives from the publisher's unique marketing strategy, which focuses on several key words and themes, *yujo* (friendship), *doryoku* (perseverance), and *shori* (victory), as well as the extensive administration of questionnaires targeting elementary and junior high school boys. The first 4.85 million copies of the 1988 New Year's special issue of this magazine sold out immediately. Since most of *Jampu's* readers (83.1 percent) are Japanese boys between the ages of ten and fifteen, it is likely that nearly seven out of every ten boys in this age bracket purchased this 1988 New Year's special issue, and *Jump's* weekly circulation exceeds 6 million copies.[6] The immense popularity of *manga* suggests that they somehow capture what is real and important in the lives of Japanese youths.

Many visitors to Japan are appalled by the violence and pornography that are often graphically depicted in *manga*, including situations of rape, bondage, sadomasochism, and voyeurism, with women nearly always the victims. For the most part, however, truly offensive *manga* are the minority, and most, though of little educational value, are quite harmless entertainment. It is well to remember here that every culture has different norms of acceptability in the arts and that *manga* derive from both *ukiyo-e* (woodblock prints) and *kibyoshi* (serialized yellow-jacket books popular among the masses in the late Edo period) in which exaggerated sexuality and stylized violence were very much a part.

Indeed, the positive influences of *manga* are quite evident. Nearly one fifth (18.2 percent) of *manga* readers feel that they are good at reading kanji, calculating numbers, and drawing pictures. Many *manga* readers (over 70 percent) work hard to excel in their studies and athletics and possess a variety of positive dreams about their future.[7]

GOALS OF JUNIOR HIGH SCHOOL STUDENTS

Japanese youths today enjoy an extremely short period of free time, and junior high school students have less free time in a day (under three hours) than all other students.[8] At the same time, *dankai* juniors today are far more relaxed than those of the previous generation.

According to a 1993 comparative survey of the Japan Youth Research Institute, eight out of ten junior high school students in Japan and the United States view "having a happy life" as a very important goal (see Figure 5–1). But American and Japanese students differ considerably on other goals such as "pursuing one's own interests," "relaxing and enjoying oneself," and "attaining a high social position." The fact that Japanese students rank all of these goals much lower than their American counterparts underscores the continued value of hard work and group-oriented over individual pursuits in Japanese society.

When compared with young people in other countries, Japanese youths show a relatively high degree of satisfaction with contemporary society (64 percent in Sweden; 64 percent in Thailand; 63 percent in Germany; 44 percent in Japan; 43 percent in the United States; 19 percent in Korea; and 5.1 percent in Russia).[9] Nevertheless, more than half (53.4 percent) express their dissatisfaction. Social problems identified by Japanese youth include gaps based on educational achievement (53.8 percent); environmental destruction (50.9 percent); and inadequate social welfare programs (50.4 percent). American young people, in comparison, are most distressed by various forms of discrimination (71.9 percent); unemployment (61.0 percent); environmental destruction (59.4 percent); poverty (58.4 percent); and the lack of respect accorded to young people's opinions (51.0 percent).[10] It is interesting to note that most Japanese youth (70 percent), as opposed to just one third (39 percent) of American youth, are unwilling to take positive actions to redress the issues of which they are most critical.[11]

LIFESTYLES OF HIGH SCHOOL STUDENTS IN JAPAN

Today's Japanese young people attend high school for two primary reasons: to advance to higher educational institutions (50 percent) and because there is nothing else to do (42 percent).[12] But despite their motivation for entering high school, all students fall victim to the fiercely competitive "examination hell" syndrome. Most, in fact, believe in the necessity of such a system. According to a study conducted by the Prime Minister's Office in 1992, approximately half of Japanese high school students view the entrance examination as "a good opportunity to review

Figure 5–1

Importance of the Goals in the Life of Junior High School Students in Japan and the United States: Proportions of Very Important

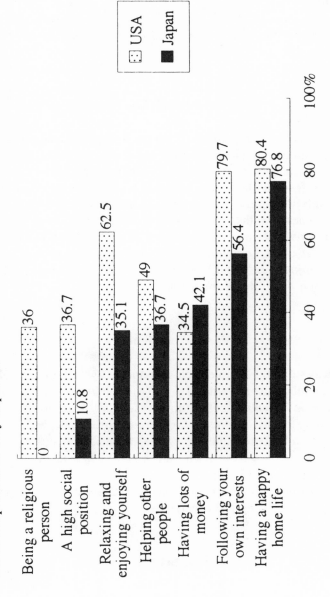

Source: Japan Youth Research Institute, 1993b, 8.

and summarize what has been learned'' and the process of preparation for the entrance examination as "contributing to self-discipline."[13]

Thus, the most striking aspect of their lifestyle is the limited time for leisure or spiritual enrichment, activities that help foster individuality and creativity. Indeed, the daily average of free time for elementary school, junior high school, and senior high school students is approximately the same as that for young workers.[14]

Attitudes toward Teachers and School

Even though Japanese high school students devote most of their time to schooling, a high proportion possess negative attitudes toward the school environment. When asked if they have teachers with whom they feel comfortable disclosing personal problems, only one third responded positively.[15] Clearly, the majority of Japanese youths maintain only casual contact with their teachers. And half of them (49.1 percent) feel that teachers do not care whether the students really understand what they teach.[16] A dismal one in ten find their classes interesting, while one third do not enjoy them at all.[17] Regarding school rules and regulations, seven out of ten deem them unnecessary.[18]

Friends

Japanese young people seem to find their greatest personal satisfaction in their relationships with friends. Most have a large number of close friends and acquaintances, although they use the terms interchangeably.[19] They like to have friends who are cheerful (96.4 percent), with whom they can talk about anything (92.8 percent), who possess a good sense of humor (91.9 percent), who are kind (89.5 percent), loyal (82.5 percent), responsible (79.6 percent), successful in school (79.0 percent), and intelligent (76.4 percent), and who have a strong sense of justice regarding right and wrong (72.8 percent).[20]

High School Dropouts

Today the number of high school dropouts in Japan is approximately 2 out of every 100 students. According to a 1993 Ministry of Education survey, the total number of high school dropouts during the 1992–1993 academic year was 101,194, representing 1.9 percent of the total high school student population. This is the lowest figure on record since the start of the survey in 1982 (106,041; 2.3 percent).[21] Nevertheless, since the 1985–1986 academic year, the total number of high school dropouts has exceeded 110,000 annually.

Students' reasons for leaving high school fall into eight basic categories: poor academic performance; ill health, injury, or death; financial reasons; personal conduct problems such as pregnancy; changes in academic programs; family problems; maladjustment to school life; and others.

In recent years, "changes in academic programs" has replaced "maladjustment to school life" as the primary reason students give for dropping out of school. Dropouts who change their academic programs have several options. They may prepare independently for the qualifying examination to enter a university, study at technical schools, or find employment. However, since no follow-up studies on high school dropouts have been conducted, their exact whereabouts are unknown exactly. In light of the acute manpower shortage in the Japanese labor market today, the Ministry of Labor has established a program (effective in spring 1991) that assists in the employment of high school dropouts.

High School Graduates Preparing for College Entrance Examinations

There are two baby boom generations in Japan: the first generation (8.06 million) born between 1947 and 1949 and the second generation (8.16 million) born to the first between 1971 and 1974. The second baby boom generation has fueled the increase in the number of *ronin* in Japan (i.e., high school graduates who fail the college entrance examination and are preparing for another try). According to the advance report of the Basic Survey on Education, of the total high school graduates in 1990, nearly half (867,000) attempted to enter higher educational institutions. In addition, 292,000 *ronin* joined the competition. Thus, while 1,159,000 youths took college entrance examinations, only 721,000 actually entered colleges and universities in the spring of 1990, leaving 438,000 *ronin*.

The number of *ronin* has steadily increased from 1986 through 1992, when the last cohort of the second baby boom generation came of age for the college entrance examination. From 1993 onward, however, as the population of eighteen-year-olds in Japan continues to decline dramatically, their annual total is projected to decrease.

The *ronin* lifestyle has a significant impact on the future of Japanese youth. High school graduates who spend one, two, and sometimes even three years studying to pass the college entrance examination are spending valuable years of their young lives memorizing useless exam information rather than forging ahead to find new life paths. This is because entrance into college is perceived as a necessary step on the way to a successful life in Japan, and those who do not get into college feel doomed to fail.

High School Students in Japan and the United States

Comparative studies of the differences in Japanese and American high school students' lifestyles in the late 1970s and in the early 1990s (see Figure 5-2) revealed quite contrasting life types.[22] In the 1970s, American high school students were generally of an "enjoy-life" type, with strong social skills such as dating, leadership, and community involvement. Japanese students were either of an "apathetic" or "study-manic" type evincing a lack of appropriate social skills.

However, changes in the lifestyles of Japanese high school students over the past twenty years have been quite striking. Today these students seem to be enjoying life more (53 percent), although their social skills remain poor (13 percent). Percentages for their American and Taiwanese counterparts in enjoyment and social skills are 35 percent/81 percent and 23 percent/58 percent, respectively. Interestingly enough, Japanese high school students today (47 percent) are less "study-maniacs" than both American students (65 percent) and Taiwanese (77 percent) but are consequently more pessimistic about their future (23 percent) as compared to their American (3 percent) and Taiwanese (7 percent) counterparts. They are quite individualistic with respect to their families (62 percent) and are more concerned about achieving a happy marital life than finding a good job (69 percent).

Another study conducted by the Japan Youth Research Institute in 1990 measured the attitudes of Japanese and American high school students toward their future. By the time they reach thirty years of age, Japanese youth would like to be employed by small- to medium-sized companies (46 percent), work in large corporations (32 percent), or have

Figure 5–2
The Degree of Agreement in Lifestyles among High School Students in Japan, the United States, and Taiwan

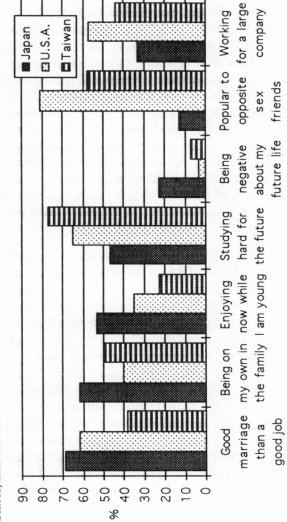

Source: Japan Youth Research Institute, 1994.

professional careers in medicine or law (13 percent). For the most part, they were not so enthusiastic about working or eager for adventure in their youth. On the other hand, American youth at thirty years of age would like to have professional careers in medicine or law (48 percent), work in large corporations (47 percent), and/or own their own companies (27 percent). They tend to have positive attitudes toward working and want great adventures before reaching thirty years of age (see Figure 5–2).

When asked about their dreams for the future, students in both countries expressed strong interest in such areas as sports (Japan: 33 percent; United States: 36 percent); academic and high-technology pursuits (Japan: 24 percent; United States: 38 percent); contributing to the nation and society (Japan: 14 percent; United States: 33 percent).[23] But in all categories, American students' hopes and dreams surpass their Japanese counterparts. Concerning the future state of the two nations, a greater proportion of both Japanese and American youths projected Japan's supremacy in the fields of science and technology, economy, and education, although Japanese students' attitudes toward their own country were much less positive.

COLLEGE STUDENTS

Today more than four out of ten Japanese youth in the college age group advance on to higher educational institutions each year. In 1993, it was 40.9 percent (38.5 percent for males and 43.4 percent for females in that age group), the first time that the proportion exceeded 40 percent.[24] These rates are among the highest of industrialized nations today, second only to the United States' 44.1 percent rate.

The percentage of female students continuing on to university has increased dramatically over the past decade, up from 5.5 percent in 1960. In the spring of 1990, for the first time in the history of Japanese education, the total number of female college entrants exceeded male entrants, although the majority of these female freshmen entered junior rather than four-year colleges.[25] The majority of male freshmen, on the other hand, entered four-year colleges and universities.

After graduation, nine out of ten Japanese female college students plan to work, but only one in five wants to start her own business or pursue a professional career. In contrast, seven out of ten female college students in America plan to start their own businesses in the future and hold executive positions.[26]

Although more than one third of Japanese youth go on to higher education, only a fraction of them regard college as a place to study and learn. This leisure-land syndrome is defined by the lack of interest in and apathetic attitudes toward thinking and learning manifested by both teachers and students.[27] A 1990 survey conducted by the Ministry of Education reveals that approximately half of Japanese college students feel that lectures are boring (49 percent for liberal arts courses; 43 percent for major courses). Obviously, little thought or effort is made to challenge these students' potential or to develop their creative thinking skills. Consequently, college students in Japan think of life and society as insignificant.

Unfortunately, the burden placed on the average Japanese family to support this leisurely college life is immense. A recent survey reveals that as much as one third (31.1 percent) of the annual Japanese household income is consumed to cover the costs of a freshman living alone and attending a private college in Tokyo.[28] In 1993, for example, the total household expenditure for entrance examinations, fees and tuitions (¥2,087,000/$20,870), and monthly allowances between April and December (¥124,600/$12,460) totaled ¥3,233,920 of an annual income of ¥10,396,000.

PROBLEMS OF JAPANESE YOUTH

Young people in Japan today evince a number of social problems. Some of these are peculiar to Japanese society, but others can be found among young people throughout the world. Four particular problems— namely, school violence, filial violence, bullying, and school phobia— have their roots in Japan's educational and family structures.

School Violence

School violence can be classified into three basic forms: violence against teachers, violence among students, and vandalism of school property. Changes in school violence over the past decade are shown in Figure 5–3a (violence cases) and Figure 5–3b (violence against teachers). Incidents of school violence have been on the rise since 1986, reaching the highest levels in 1992–1993 (3,666 cases in junior high schools; 1,594 cases in senior high schools). Although school violence in Japan

Figure 5–3
**Changes in the Number of Schools and Teachers Having School Violence
Problems: 1982–1992**

Figure 5-3a. School Violence

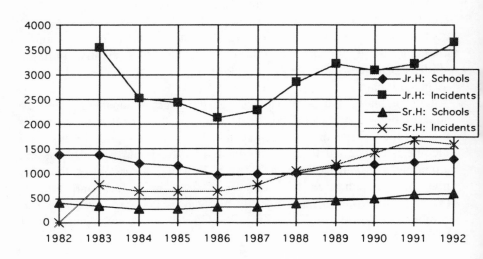

Figure 5-3b. Violence against Teachers

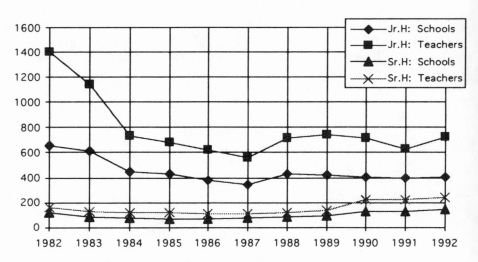

Source: Ministry of Education, 1993e, 6–7, tables 2–1 and 2–2.

occurs more frequently in junior high schools (1,293 cases) than in senior high schools (590 cases), the difference in rate of occurrence is minimal (12.2 percent of junior high schools and 14.2 percent of senior high schools.)[29] The reason for this is partly because there are approximately 2.5 times as many public junior high schools as public senior high schools in Japan (10,596 versus 4,166).

In general, incidents of school violence have occurred consistently across the three major categories, suggesting a general outcry against the school environment as a whole. In most cases, the problem students are those who do not fit into the study-oriented environment of the Japanese education system.

Filial Violence

Interestingly enough, it is the students who do well in school who most frequently engage in acts of filial violence, that is, violent acts against members of their immediate family, including parents, siblings, or grandparents. Since such violence is carried out within the privacy of families, it is extremely difficult to detect. Sometimes the problems are brought to the attention of the police, mental institutions, and school-teachers, but only when the parents become particularly desperate. The abusive conduct of children against parents has even resulted in such extreme forms of abuse as patricide and matricide.

Public exposure of private problems is quite alien to Japanese tradition, and keeping family problems within the family is considered a virtue. Consequently, filial violence has only recently been recognized as a pressing social problem in Japan—and an indication of the maladjustment of youth to diverse social and cultural norms in rapidly changing Japanese society.[30]

Changing attitudes among the general public toward filial violence emerged most clearly in the wake of four incidents of murder: a Kaisei High School student in 1977, a grandmother in 1979, and a mother and father in 1980 and 1990. These four incidents were widely reported for two reasons. First, the four adolescent boys charged had attended top-notch Japanese prep schools. Second, the four incidents involved murder/suicides within the family. Although many incidents of filial violence continue to go unreported in Japan today, these cases may have helped more parents to speak openly about the problem and to seek public assistance.[31] In 1988, the Japanese Police Agency received 860 reports of filial violence, an increase of 7.8 percent over the previous year.

There are three basic types of filial violence: (1) acts of violence intended to physically hurt another person, including beating, kicking, and shoving; (2) acts of violence against objects, such as throwing things, destroying furniture, tearing clothes, and setting fires; (3) verbal violence, such as screaming, hissing, booing, and jeering. The victims of such violent acts are often seriously injured and must receive extended medical and/or psychological treatment.

Two nationwide surveys on filial violence have revealed that 80 percent of these abusive adolescents are found among fifteen-year-old or sixteen-year-old males.[32] Primary victims are most frequently the mothers of the offenders. Socioeconomic backgrounds of the parents tend to be quite high, and the violent youth frequently attend respected public or private schools. But the peer relationships of these violent adolescents are poor, and they tend to lack normal social skills.

Homes experiencing filial violence are typically characterized by a dominating mother and the psychological absence of the father. The mother's overindulgence and overprotection make it difficult for the abusive youth to attain emotional independence. These youth retain such a strong sense of self-identification with the family that they strive to conceal their problems from nonfamily members. Outside the home, these children are well behaved; it is only inside the home that they become violent.

The nature of filial violence in Japan seems somehow linked to a conflict between the individual characteristics of Japanese youth and the structural elements of Japanese society and family. Struggling to attain a healthy psychological separation from their parents, these children see violence as the only means to express themselves and to restore communication with other members of their family. This distortion of family dynamics suggests that Japan's rigid social structure may, in some cases, be preventing the normal development of Japanese youth.

Bullying

Another pressing problem among Japanese youth is *ijime*, or student bullying, which sometimes results in suicides by the victims or homicides by the offenders. This abusive conduct has three characteristics: First, it occurs between a strong abuser and a feeble victim who cannot or will not fight back; second, the physical and/or psychological abuses are continuous in nature; and third, school authorities are aware of the abuse because the victims report it.

Owing to the efforts of all concerned, bullying has declined over the last few years across most school levels. These decreases notwithstanding, a total of 23,258 incidents of bullying were reported in the 1992–1993 academic year. Such incidents occurred most frequently at junior high schools (13,632 cases, 32.5 percent of the total cases in public high schools), followed by elementary schools (7,300 cases, 11.8 percent) and senior high schools (2,326 cases, 23.6 percent). Today bullying occurs in one third of public junior high schools in Japan.[33]

The most frequent forms of bullying are teasing, physical abuse, verbal aggression, and ostracism. Incidents of physical abuse increase with the students' age, occurring most frequently at senior high schools, followed by junior high schools and then by elementary schools. It is usually the case that victims are abused by offenders in the same age group.

Most Japanese agree that the reasons for bullying derive from problems within the family or from the interrelationship between victim, family, school, and society.[34] Japan's materialistic advancement has not included the psychological and subjective dimensions of nurturing that are essential for proper adolescent development, reflecting the opposing elements of tradition and modernity in Japanese society.

Although bullying has occurred down through the ages, incidents of being bullied to death or committing suicide because of bullying have been relatively recent, particularly among children of the 1947–1949 baby boom generation. These baby boom parents, struggling in a society of intense competition and liberated by a number of social movements, have developed new concepts of family life and parenting that are somehow deficient in providing children with the love, affection, and discipline they need for proper emotional development.[35] In consequence, Japanese youth today have turned into offenders and victims of bullying.

School Phobia

Today it is not uncommon for children to rebel against attending school, and a growing number suffer from school phobia, in which they reject school and confine themselves to life within the family.

Despite real declines in the number of Japanese children currently attending school, the number of elementary and junior high schools who suffer from school phobia has been increasing over the past few decades; truancy at elementary schools has more than doubled, and at junior high schools, it has more than tripled.[36] The number of students absent from

school for more than fifty days was higher for both elementary and junior
high school students in the 1992–1993 academic year than in any other
year after 1966–1967 when the Ministry of Education first initiated this
survey. Cases of extended absenteeism increased from 4,430 to 10,449
for elementary school students and from 12,286 to 47,526 for junior high
school students between 1966 and 1992.

Over the last ten years, reported incidents of school phobia among
elementary school students has more than doubled, and among junior
high school students, it has more than tripled, with actual numbers pur-
ported to be even greater.

Causes of school phobia are difficult to pinpoint, but maladjustment
to school life, juvenile delinquency, peer problems, grade problems, and
problems at home are no doubt among them. In fact, in a 1993 survey
by the Ministry of Education, school officials reported that dissatisfaction
with the school environment (i.e., peer relations, teacher-student relations, pressure for studying, etc.) accounted for one third (37.7 percent)
of all cases of school phobia, followed closely by personal problems
(31.3 percent) and problems at home (23.7 percent).[37] In the first study
of its kind, the Ministry of Education recently interviewed truant students, their parents, and school officials concerning the possible causes
of the problem. Whereas most students attributed the problem to the
school environment (44.5 percent), followed by personal problems (27.8
percent) and problems at home (14.8 percent), school officials most frequently blamed problems at home (43.2 percent). Parents, on the other
hand, found personal problems (33.9 percent) to be the primary cause.[38]
These contradictory results indicate important perceptional differences
among the three parties concerning the causes of school phobia.

In an effort to alleviate the growing problem of school phobia, the
Ministry of Health and Welfare established a "mental friend" program
in the spring of 1991. The mental friend program is similar to "big
brother" and "big sister" programs in the United States. Through volunteer counseling by college students still of an age to relate to the
problems of Japanese youth, younger students are encouraged to disclose
their personal inhibitions about school and, it is hoped, to overcome
them.[39]

As with many other problems afflicting Japanese youth, however, the
fundamental solution must come through a reevaluation of Japan's educational system and family support structures. The gap between objective training and spiritual, subjective nurturing both at school and at

home has made it virtually impossible for some Japanese children to grow up in a normal and acceptable manner.

NOTES

1. Of the total Japanese population in 1993 (124,760,000), 15.44 percent were between the ages of fifteen and twenty-four (fifteen to nineteen: 9,624,000, or 7.73 percent; and twenty to twenty-four: 9,594,000, or 7.71 percent); Statistics Bureau of the Management and Coordination Agency, 1994, 20, table 2.

2. Chikushi, 1986, 291–294.

3. Nakano, 1988.

4. Oda, 1990, 70–71.

5. The popularity of *manga* even on serious topics is exemplified by Ishinomori's series of hardcover comic books that teach readers about economics (1986–1988). Its first three volumes, each about 300 pages long, have had combined sales of 1.5 million copies, and volume four, published in April 1988, was equally well received (Otsuka, 1988, 287). Volume one of *Manga Nihon Keizai Nyumon* (A Cartoon Introduction to the Japanese Economy) by Shotaro Ishinomori is available in English translation entitled *Japan, Inc.: An Introduction to Japanese Economics (The Comic Book)* (1988).

6. Otsuka, 1988, 287; *Japan Economic Journal*, 1993d.

7. *Japan Economic Journal*, 1993d. A questionnaire survey was conducted in Chiba prefecture during the summer of 1992. A total of 1,256 fourth- and sixth-grade elementary and junior high school students responded.

8. *Japan Economic Journal*, 1993i.

9. Management and Coordination Agency, Office of Youth, 1994, 62–63, figures 5–9 and 5–10. "Comparative Studies on the Attitudes of Youth" have been conducted since 1972. This was the fifth study of those in eleven countries (Japan, the United States, United Kingdom, Germany, France, Switzerland, Korea, the Philippines, Thailand, Brazil, and Russia). In the spring of 1993, approximately 1,000 young men and women between the ages of eighteen and twenty-four were interviewed in each country.

10. Ibid., 63–65, figures 5–11 and 5–12.

11. Ibid., 59–61, table 5–1, figure 5–7.

12. Ministry of Education, 1994b; Kumagai, 1988c, 2.

13. Prime Minister's Office, 1993f.

14. Ibid.

15. Youth Bureau of the Management and Coordination Agency, 1985, reported in 1990g, 77–78.

16. NHK Broadcasting Culture Research Institute, 1987, reported in ibid.

17. Youth Bureau of the Management and Coordination Agency, 1988, reported in ibid., 81.

18. Ibid., 82–83.

19. Popular answers were having six to nine close friends (26.2 percent), three to five (23 percent), more than twenty (20.6 percent), ten to fourteen (17.2 percent), and fifteen to nineteen (7.1 percent). A few (4 percent) had only one to two close friends, and 2 out of 100 (1.9 percent) had no close friends at all. Youth Bureau of the Management and Coordination Agency, 1988, reported in ibid., 107.

20. Japan Youth Research Institute, 1993a.

21. Ministry of Education, 1994a, 5–6, table 3.

22. Kumagai, 1979c; 1988c; K. Takeuchi, 1980.

23. Japan Youth Research Institute, 1994, 19–23.

24. Ministry of Education, 1993a.

25. Ministry of Education, 1990.

26. The survey on "female college students' attitudes and consumer behaviors" was conducted by the *Nikkei Ryutsu Shimbun* (Japan Economic Journal Service Industries) in November 1989.

27. Iwata, 1985; Kumagai, 1988c, 126–127; Ogose, 1988.

28. Association of Colleges and Universities in the Greater Tokyo Metropolitan Area, 1994. During the months of May and June, parents whose children entered colleges and universities in April 1993 in Tokyo or one of the five adjacent prefectures received questionnaires through the mail; 10,400 households replied.

29. Prime Minister's Office, 1993f; Ministry of Education, 1993e: 5–17.

30. Analysis of filial violence from a sociological point of view was initiated by Enomoto, who suggested the necessity to analyze the phenomenon as an emerging social problem in Japan rather than to treat it as a pathological aberration (Enomoto, 1973).

31. Inamura, 1980; Kumagai, 1981a, 1981b.

32. Kumagai, 1983a, 173–194. This article analyzes two nationwide studies on filial violence in Japan, one by the Youth Development Headquarters (1980) of 1,057 abusive adolescents and the other by the Japanese Police Agency (1981) of 1,025 battering youths.

33. Ministry of Education, 1993e, 21–30.

34. Prime Minister's Office, 1986, 12–14.

35. Kumagai, 1988c, 100–101.

36. Ministry of Education, 1993e, 31–43.

37. Ibid., 37.

38. Ministry of Education, 1993b, 8.

39. *Japan Economic Journal*, 1990g.

PART III

WOMEN AND LABOR FORCE PARTICIPATION

CHAPTER 6

The Changing Status of Women

MODERNIZATION VERSUS TRADITIONAL IMAGES OF JAPANESE WOMEN

Despite Japan's high levels of economic, industrial, and technological development, the status of women in Japanese society is not yet on par with that of women in Western industrial nations. One of the primary reasons for their continued inferiority can be found in the way that Japan's modernization process has occurred; radical changes in women's legal rights were imposed from above (i.e., by the American occupation forces), while traditional mores regarding women's place in society have been slow in changing. Therefore, despite the many laws that give women the legal right to equality at home, at work, and in politics, the reality is somewhat different.

JAPANESE WOMEN IN THE PREMODERN ERA[1]

In ancient and medieval times, women enjoyed a position of relative equality, if not authority and power, vis-à-vis men in Japanese society. Evidence of matrilineal descent and matriarchal authority in Japan predates the patriarchal family of the seventh century, and during the Heian period of the eleventh and twelfth centuries, husbands and wives held and disposed of property independently. Husbands would sometimes leave property to their wives, but wives generally left their property to their children. Property inheritance by women in aristocratic classes was common until as late as the fourteenth century.

Examples of the high status of Japanese women in aristocratic society can be found in two of the oldest pieces of literature written by women, namely, *Genji Monogatari* (Tale of Prince Genji) by Murasaki Shikibu and *Makura no Soshi* (Pillow Story) by Seisho Nagon. There are also examples from history of Japanese women in powerful provincial families engaging in money lending and the production, sale, and storage of rice, and women in the Middle Ages were known to have controlling interest in *za* (commercial monopolies somewhat like guilds) for fans, salt, and articles of clothing. Even in marriage, women enjoyed relative equality in property rights and membership in village communal organizations.

The gradual subordination of Japanese women occurred over the centuries and is most directly related to the establishment of the traditional family system, which is based on patriarchal authority. In the Nara and Heian periods, it was common for husbands and wives to maintain separate residences, or for the wife's family to adopt the husband as a son. But later, when wives began to join their husbands' families, granting property to a daughter who would eventually leave the family meant handing over part of the family estate to another family. Thus, women's inheritance rights were directly and negatively affected by measures to protect the family unit. By the end of the sixteenth century, women also lost rights to commercial property, and the old *za* were disbanded.

Patriarchal authority became firmly established during the early Edo period, when "the ruling warrior class forced the *ie* system of social organization on the peasantry as a control mechanism for tax collection purposes and to keep order. Single inheritance soon became the norm."[2] After the Meiji Restoration, when the *ie* system was enforced legally throughout Japan, the male head of household assumed full legal authority for all family members. The 1898 Civil Code favored the husband in marriage, property rights, and other aspects of family law. Adultery constituted legal grounds for divorce only if committed by the wife, and fathers retained custody of the children in all cases of divorce. In the event of her husband's death, the wife came under the authority of the eldest son, thus following the Confucian dictum that a woman should in youth obey her father, in maturity her husband, and in old age her son. Some have argued that it was this Confucian philosophy and the long feudal experience of Japan that combined to restrict the freedom of women and force them into complete subordination to men.[3]

JAPANESE WOMEN IN PEASANT SOCIETY

In the family structure of peasant society, all family members were regarded as assets, and peasant women were considered coworkers of men in the fields throughout the Edo and Meiji periods. Female property rights were retained until the seventeenth century, and division of labor was one of "negotiable responsibility and shifting allocation of duties."[4] During this period, it was not uncommon for a peasant woman, of her own choosing, to divorce and remarry three or four times. Thus, women in farm families had considerably more power and authority than those in upper-class families.[5]

One of the greatest ironies of Japan's social modernization process is that it lowered the status of women in the peasant classes and made all women, regardless of class, inferior to the men in their households.

POSTWAR CHANGES IN THE STATUS OF JAPANESE WOMEN

The Constitution of 1947, enacted under the directorship of the American occupation following Japan's defeat in World War II, laid the groundwork for the democratization of Japanese women. Discrimination in political, economic, or social relations because of race, creed, sex, social status, or family origin was forbidden (Article 14). Women's equality in family life was guaranteed by laws founded from the standpoint of individual dignity and the essential equality of the sexes (Article 24), granting both husband and wife equal rights with regard to choice of spouse, property, inheritance, place of domicile, divorce, and other matters related to marriage and the family. With the enactment of the new Civil Code in 1947, the family system in Japan underwent further change: Male household headship was abolished, and the family unit was defined to include only husband, wife, and children. Additional political, educational, and workplace reforms gave women the rights to vote, to be educated on an equal footing with men, and to receive equal pay for equal work.

Although equality for women in political, economic, and social relations has been guaranteed by law for more than fifty years now, the continued secondary status of Japanese women suggests that traditional mores concerning the roles of women in society are more powerful than legal sanctions.

JAPANESE WOMEN IN POLITICS AND PUBLIC ADMINISTRATION

The Political Awakening

The year 1989 has been heralded as the epoch-making year for Japanese women's political consciousness, clearly demonstrating that voting women are a force to be reckoned with. In the House of Councilors election in July of that year, the ruling Liberal-Democratic Party (LDP) lost its majority rule, securing only 36 of the 126 contested seats and ending with just 109 of the 252 total seats in the House. The Japan Socialist Party (JSP), led by Chairwoman Takako Doi, increased its representation by 24 seats, 11 of which went to women. An additional 22 women were elected from other opposition parties, making a total of 33 women councilors or 13.1 percent of the House of Councilors' 252 seats.

The primary reason for the LDP's 1989 defeat was its passage of a 3 percent consumption tax on everything from children's snacks to school supplies and maternity expenses. Enacted on April 1, 1989, the tax forged a direct link between domestic life and national politics. Women, who hold the purse strings in Japanese families, were particularly angered by the tax, well aware of just how cruel the across-the-board 3 percent consumption tax was for society's weakest members, such as the elderly and women heading single-parent households.[6]

Following the LDP's massive defeat, male critics who openly supported the LDP began an undisguised attack on women seeking a life in politics. Questioning women's ability to become useful participants in the political process, feature articles appeared in Japan's weekly magazines predicting that women's new-found political clout would be the death of Japan.[7] Popular phrases such as *obatarian* (created by writer Katsuhiko Hotta in his comic portrayal of the daily activities of middle-aged Japanese women) and "madonna" power were used to scorn the life of middle-aged Japanese women seeking to make a difference in the society in which they live. Political equality may be the law in Japan, but the reality for women in politics is clearly somewhat different.

Prime Minister Kiichi Miyazawa's forced resignation in the summer of 1993 resulted in a second political awakening in Japan. Not only did the LDP lose its majority in the House of Representatives for the first time in nearly four decades, but Takako Doi, former chairwoman of the JSP, was elected as Speaker of the House. She was the first woman ever to pursue this position. Former Prime Minister Morihiro Hosokawa's Unified Coalition Cabinet (composed of eight non-LDP parties) was the first in Japanese history to include three women at one time. With the recognition of the contribution that women could make in the political arena, it was strongly hoped that these changes would bring a new-found political consciousness to the Japanese people and to women in particular.

Under the current government led by Prime Minister Murayama, political reform is expected to continue. Nevertheless, given Hosokawa's and Hata's very brief terms in office, questions remain concerning the degree to which political consciousness among Japanese women was actually raised. Perhaps an even truer form of political awakening among Japanese women will take place in the years to come.

Voting Rates

Japanese women voted and ran for public office for the first time on April 10, 1946. In the early history of postwar national elections, there was a gap of more than 10 percent between the voting rates of women and men.[8] Over the years, however, the gap began to close, and in the 1968 House of Councilors election, the voting rate of women (69.0 percent) exceeded for the first time that of men (68.9 percent). Thereafter, the women's voting rate has consistently exceeded the rate for men, however slightly.

In the July 1992 House of Councilors election, the nationwide voting rate was as low as 50.72 percent (50.5 percent for men versus 50.86 percent for women). In the July 1993 House of Representatives election, the total voting rate was 67.27 percent (66.41 percent for men versus 68.09 percent for women). Given the overwhelming public concern for political reform among men and women alike, these voting rates were surprisingly low.

Similar trends in voting rates can be observed at the prefectural, city, town, and village levels, called *toitsu chiho senkyo* or nationwide local elections. Until the early 1960s, voting rates for women were lower than their male counterparts' rates. Thereafter, however, voting rates for women continued to exceed those for men. In the most recent elections held in 1991, for example, voting rates of women exceeded those of men at all levels (prefectures: 62.40 percent versus 58.45 percent; cities: 68.13 percent versus 62.45 percent; towns and villages: 88.23 percent versus 84.34 percent).[9]

It is interesting to note that the lower the level of election, the higher the voting rate for both women and men. In fact, differences in the voting rates between the prefectural and town/village levels were as high as 26 percent for both sexes in the last nationwide local elections. Japanese people, and women in particular, are more anxious to take part in local elections, since the results of these elections have a much greater impact on their daily lives.

The fact that nearly nine out of ten Japanese women in towns and villages voted in the 1991 elections may also reflect, in some sense, the traditional nature of Japanese society. At this level, it is easy to identify those who do not vote, and this may be held against them. And in some cases, if the locality is small enough, how one votes may also be easily determined. Thus, high voting rates at the local level may be more the result of conforming to traditional expectations of human relationships than an indication of the political awakening of Japanese women.

Women Holding Political Office

Despite their obvious interest in politics, women in public office have been consistently underrepresented. As of the end of 1989, women held only 7 of the 500 seats (1.4 percent) in the House of Representatives. In February 1990, 12 women (2.3 percent) were elected to this House, nearing the number of women elected in the first general election under the new Constitution in 1949 (2.4 percent). Combined with their 33 seats in the House of Councilors, women officeholders constituted only 5.9 percent of the total membership of both Houses in 1990, a significant gain over their 4 percent level prior to July 1989 but still abysmally low.

Step by step, further progress is being made, at least at the national level. As a result of the July 1992 House of Councilors election, women came to occupy 37 seats (14.7 percent of 252 seats, with 1 female councilor added later, yielding 15.1 percent of the total seats), and in the recent July 1993 national election of the House of Representatives, 14 women were elected (2.7 percent of 511 seats). Combining both Houses, women now hold 52 of a total 763 seats (6.8 percent).

At the local level, however, women's representation in public office is much lower (3.3 percent of total membership in all local-level assemblies). At the end of 1992, women held only 2.8 percent of total membership in prefectural assemblies, 5.8 percent in city assemblies, and 2.0 percent in town/village assemblies.[10] It is surprising to note that women hold the fewest seats in town/village assemblies, since the voting rates of women have been the highest at this level, usually about 90 percent.

Given the continued dominance of men in the Japanese political world, cabinet appointments for women have been extremely rare. In light of societal pressures, the prime minister's cabinet formed after the House of Councilors election in July 1989 included women in two important ministerial posts: Chief Cabinet Secretary and the Head of the Economic Planning Agency. However, when a new cabinet was formed in February 1990 only six months after their appointments, these women were replaced by male politicians. General opinion has it that these women ministers were simply used in the political game to give the Japanese public the impression that LDP leaders were liberated enough to welcome women as political partners.

But the revolutionary changes that have been taking place in Japanese politics since the summer of 1993 bode well for women, particularly with respect to cabinet positions. Prime Minister Hosokawa appointed three of his twenty-two cabinet positions and two of his deputy ministerial positions to women: minister of education, director of the Economic Planning Agency, director of the Environmental Protection Agency, deputy director of the Management and Coordination Agency, and deputy minister of the Science and Engineering Agency. The fact that women came to head such important governmental offices as education, economy, and environment brought a recognition of the importance of women in public administration never before seen.

With the termination of the Hosokawa cabinet, newly elected Prime Minister Hata appointed two of his twenty cabinet positions to women: minister of education and the new appointment of director of the Environmental Planning Agency. Unfortunately, because the Hata cabinet comprised representatives of minority parties only, it faced numerous difficulties in the policy-making process and was short-lived. The newly formed Murayama cabinet, composed of both LDP and Socialist Party members, included only one female cabinet position, that of minister of the Science and Engineering Agency.

Although it is encouraging to see that more and more women are assuming public-elected and appointed positions in Japan, it is obvious that men continue to dominate the political scene. In fact, during the recent formation of Japan's leading coalition party, one influential male politician stated that coalition formation should have nothing to do with which women men decide to sleep. Such discriminatory attitudes reveal that women continue to be treated as sex objects rather than as serious colleagues in the political arena.

The equal right to vote, bestowed on all Japanese people regardless of class or sex under the American occupation, was an important step in paving the way for the political emancipation of women. But the long road that followed, and the equally long road that still lies ahead, constitutes a struggle against Japanese traditional mores that no law imposed from above could ever erase. Women's liberalization must begin with a political awakening among men.

SEX ROLES

Men at Work and Women at Home

Attitudes toward traditional sex roles, epitomized in beliefs like "a man's place is at work and a woman's place is in the home" have been changing over the years (see Figure 6–1). In 1979, seven out of ten Japanese women polled (70.1 percent) agreed with this statement, but by 1992 only half (55.6 percent) did. Progress can also be observed in men's attitudes toward traditional sex roles, although it has not been as fast as that for women. In 1979, nearly eight out of ten Japanese men polled (75.6 percent) agreed that "a woman's place is in the home," but by 1992 the number had dropped to 65.7 percent.[11] Concerning their hopes for liberalization of sex roles by the year 2000, nearly four out of ten Japanese polled in 1992 (38.6 percent) looked forward to equality, including as many as 47.1 percent of men in their fifties and 48.3 percent of women in their thirties.[12]

Attitudes toward Marriage and Work

Traditionally, the majority of Japanese women in the labor force were single, but today 60.4 percent are married.[13] This turnaround has come

Figure 6–1
Changes in Attitudes toward "Men's Place Is at Work and Women's Place Is at Home":
1979–1992

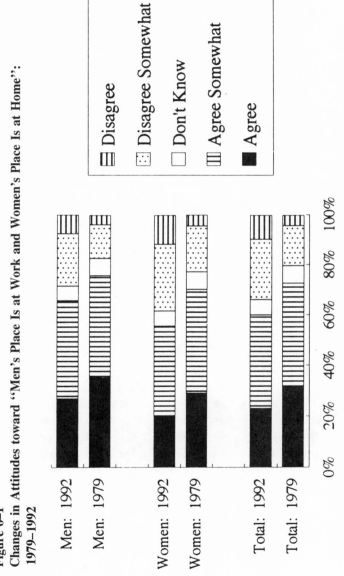

Source: Prime Minister's Office, 1993a, 43, table 6.

on the heels of a substantial increase in the average age of working women (from 26.3 years in 1960 to 36.0 years in 1992).[14] In addition, more and more newly married women are continuing to work after marriage, an increase of 13 percent between the years 1982 and 1991.[15]

Despite this obvious change in attitudes toward marriage and work, the majority of married women in Japan (59 percent) still believe that they should discontinue working once they give birth to their first child, then return to the labor force only after the completion of child rearing.[16] And additional surveys reveal that two thirds of the respondents aged thirty to sixty-nine years supported ''women's participation in the labor force, as long as it does not interfere with domestic work.''[17]

Several factors contribute to a Japanese woman's decision to remain in the full-time labor force after marriage:

- Personal motivation and commitment to work based on the time and resources invested in education and training.

- Her husband's attitude toward having a wife participating full-time in the workforce.

- Existence of a support network and/or assistance at home from a husband or other close relatives.

The presence or absence of one or more of these conditions may create a set of real-life circumstances that differ from a woman's ideal wish to remain in the labor force after marriage.

The question of whether or not to have a family is another serious consideration for married women who work. Statistics indicate that Japanese women are not only marrying much later than they used to but are having their first child much later also.[18] In fact, women with college educations who hold career-track jobs have been delaying childbirth until their early thirties.[19] These women typically graduate from college at age twenty-two, work for a few years, get married, and continue to pursue their careers. A leave of absence for a few years to bear and rear children can be detrimental, particularly at the start of a career. Therefore, these women are more likely to wait until their careers are more firmly established to have their first child. Given this growing trend toward delayed childbirth, the Japan Gynecological Association has modified its definition of *korei shosanfu* (a woman having her first child at a late age) to thirty-five years of age from the previous thirty years. But the social climate in Japan concerning married working women and childbirth has not yet been liberated. In this area, perhaps more than any other, Japanese men and women tend to adhere to traditional sex role identifications.

Sex Role Differentiation at Home

A 1991 survey by the Prime Minister's Office revealed that in Japanese households most of the work is still done by the wife/mother: cleaning/laundry, 91.3 percent; meal preparation, 91.5 percent; washing dishes, 84.7 percent; paying the bills, 83.8 percent; and grocery shopping, 84.9 percent. Although there is evidence of joint husband-wife participation in such activities as child disciplining (39.0 percent), supervising children's studies (27.8 percent), and caring for elderly parents (29.6 percent), one half of the respondents still regarded these areas as the wife's responsibility.[20]

Some observers of Japanese family life argue that wives wield a great deal of power in the home, pointing out that husbands hand over paychecks to their wives, who then manage the household budget as they see fit. But the typical Japanese wife actually has limited options for saving or spending that money. As keeper of the purse, she is simply freeing her husband of the routine secretarial task of paying the bills.

There obviously remains a clear division of labor by sex in the Japanese household today. The concept of equality in a marriage partnership may exist on the surface, but traditional ideology continues to define the Japanese woman's role in the home.

Husband-Wife Relationships

Japanese marriages, in general, still emphasize the sanctity of the institution over the value of true love and companionship. Most Japanese husbands identify the benefits of marriage as being "socially accepted as independent" and "able to depend on wives to manage their everyday life." Japanese wives identify the principal gain of marriage as "economic stability."[21]

While a great majority of husbands (94.2 percent) and wives (86.2 percent) express satisfaction with their marital life, more than a quarter of husbands (28.7 percent) and more than four in every ten wives (43.1 percent) have seriously considered divorce at one time or another during their married life. Major reasons given include incompatibility and conflicting values. Husbands are frustrated with nonunderstanding wives, and wives are dissatisfied with workaholic husbands. But most of these couples stay together for the sake of the children. Other reasons for husbands include fear of the social stigma attached to divorce (22.6 percent) and the inconvenience of single life (21.4 percent). Many wives do not divorce out of fear of financial difficulties (30.4 percent).

Although difficult to detect, there are many cases of battered wives throughout Japan. In a 1992 survey of 795 women, nearly 8 in every 10 attested to some form of physical, psychological, and/or sexual abuse by their husbands. Specific forms of abuse included pouring boiling water into their ears while they slept and being locked out of the house naked on fiercely cold nights.[22]

A growing number of battered wives have been seeking solace in shelters where they are free of their abusive husbands. The majority of battered wives that seek such temporary shelter are full-time housewives who are completely dependent on their husbands financially. Eight out of ten wives in such shelters are accompanied by their children, and some 75 percent have a repeated history of leaving their husbands.[23]

A survey conducted by the *Japan Economic Journal* in 1993 reveals, not surprisingly, that Japanese husbands and wives are not truly integrated with each other; they are *dosho imu* (sleeping in the same bed but having different dreams).[24] At the same time, both husbands and wives desire to grow together in the marriage relationship and be devoted to each other. Foremost of the wishes of wives is that their husbands respect their independent lives, and foremost for husbands is mind-to-mind communication with their wives. The conflict between the modern-day expectations of marriage partners in Japan and the reality of their circumstances reveals the ongoing struggle between tradition and modernity in Japanese society.

NOTES

1. This section draws heavily on Janet Nelson's unpublished paper "The Effects of Modernization upon the Lives of Japanese Women," 1984.
2. Wakita, 1984, 96.
3. Reischauer, 1988, 176.
4. Smith, 1981, 269.
5. Toda, 1926.
6. Sawachi, 1989, 381–385.
7. Ibid, 385.

8. In the 1946 House of Representatives election the rate for women was 67.0 percent as opposed to 78.5 percent for men; for the 1947 House of Councilors election, rates were 54.0 percent for women and 68.4 percent for men. From Asahi, 1994.

9. Prime Minister's Office, 1993e, 39, table 3–1–3.

10. Prime Minister's Office, 1993a, 39, table 3–1–4.

11. Ibid., 43–44, figure 6, table 25. In November 1992, 5,000 males and females twenty years and over were interviewed throughout Japan, with a response rate of 70.5 percent (3,524 interviews).

12. Prime Minister's Office, 1992a, 65–66, table 23. In November 1991, 3,000 males and females aged twenty and over were interviewed throughout Japan, with an interview rate of 71.2 percent.

13. Women's Bureau of the Ministry of Labor, 1993b, supplementary table 16.

14. Ibid., supplementary table 21.

15. Statistical Bureau of the Ministry of Health and Welfare, 1992, 7, table 6.

16. Ibid., 12, table 14.

17. Statistics Bureau of the Management and Coordination Agency, 1990, 12.

18. *Japan Economic Journal*, 1992.

19. The average age at first marriage for Japanese women in 1991 was 25.7 years; for those with college educations, it was as high as 27.3 years. Statistical Bureau of the Ministry of Health and Welfare, 1992, 4, table 3.

20. Prime Minister's Office, 1993a, 17–37, figure 2.

21. *Japan Economic Journal*, 1993b.

22. *Japan Economic Journal, 1994f.*

23. *Ibid.*

24. *Japan Economic Journal*, 1993.

CHAPTER 7

Japanese Women in the Workforce

STRUCTURAL CHANGES AND LABOR FORCE PARTICIPATION RATES

Throughout the process of Japanese modernization, women have constituted more than one third of the labor force, and the number of working women aged fifteen years or older has remained more or less half the total population: 53.4 percent in 1920; 48.6 percent in 1950; and 50.7 percent in 1992.[1] In 1992, 40.7 percent of the labor force was female.[2]

Although female labor participation rates have remained relatively constant over the years, the distribution of working women across industries has changed dramatically. As Figure 7–1 indicates, a complete reversal in the pattern of female labor force participation has emerged in Japan. That is, Japanese women are leaving the primary industry and moving into the tertiary industry.[3] Between 1920 and 1955, the majority of Japanese women worked in primary industry. Since 1955, however, this proportion has been declining drastically, reaching a record low of only one in every ten working women today. Conversely, the proportion of women working in secondary and tertiary industries has been increasing over the years, reaching 27.1 percent and 65.1 percent, respectively, in 1992.

Figure 7–1
Changes in Labor Force Participation Rates: 1920–1992

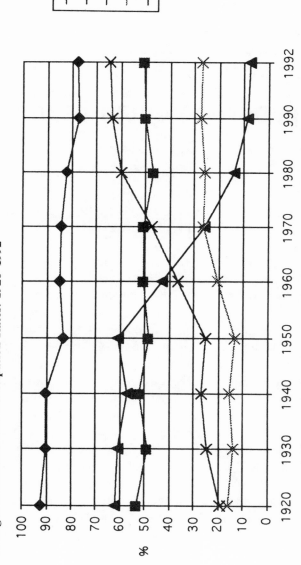

Sources: For 1920–1955: Japan Statistics Bureau, Population Census of Japan; 1920, 1930, 1940, 1947, 1950, and 1955, reported in Yano-Kota Memorial Society, 1986, 52, table 2–15. For 1960–1992: Japan Statistics Bureau, Annual Reports on the Labor Force Survey, 1960, 1965, 1970, 1975, 1980, 1985, 1990, and 1992, reported in Women's Bureau of the Ministry of Labor, 1993, appendix 7.

These structural changes in women's labor force participation rates coincide with patterns of change in the overall Japanese labor force as well as in male labor force participation rates, as discussed earlier in the current study (see Figure I–2). These changes occurred as economic growth accelerated in postwar Japanese society, creating a highly industrialized, technologically intense and computerized state. In consequence, the demand for female workers in technologically advanced and service-oriented industries grew. Since these jobs typically required a higher level of education, it is not surprising to find that the proportion of Japanese women advancing from primary to secondary education increased significantly, from 36.7 percent in 1950 to 97.2 percent in 1993. Similarly, more and more Japanese women are continuing on to higher education. Compared to a mere 5.0 percent in 1955, now some 42.4 percent of Japanese women are graduating from two-and four-year colleges.[4]

FEMALE LABOR FORCE PARTICIPATION RATES
BY AGE

Examination of female labor force participation rates according to age group provides a clearer picture of the change in Japanese women's workforce participation.

Figure 7–2 presents the proportions of Japanese women in the labor force by age in 1960, 1970, 1980 and 1990. Four distinct patterns may be discerned. First, labor force participation rates of Japanese women in the fifteen- to nineteen-years age bracket have been declining continuously. Today less than one in every five women in this age group enters the workforce.[5] This decline clearly coincides with the increase in the number of young Japanese women who are receiving a high school education. High school students are typically between fifteen and eighteen years of age.

Second, labor force participation rates of Japanese women in eight different age brackets ranging from twenty to fifty-nine years have increased continuously over the last four decades. Of the total number of women in the labor force in 1992 (26.79 million), proportions were highest for women in their early forties (14.4 percent), followed by women in their early twenties (13.2 percent).

Third, rates of increase from 1955 to 1992 are most outstanding for middle-aged working women between the ages of forty and fifty-four

Figure 7–2

Changes in Labor Force Participation Rates of Japanese Women by Age: 1960, 1970, 1980, and 1990

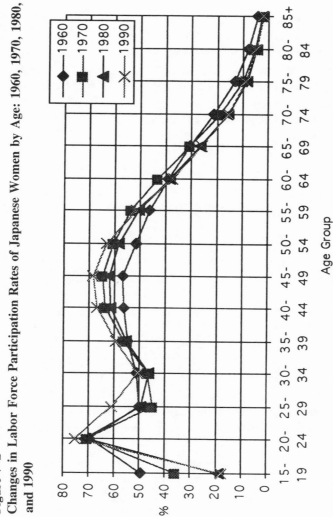

Source: Japan Statistics Bureau, Annual Reports on the Labor Force Survey, reported in the Institute of Population Problems, 1993a, 103, table 8–2.

years. In 1992, seven out of ten (70.0 percent) of these women were in the labor force (9.92 million women workers out of the 14.18 million total women population for the relevant cohorts).[6]

Fourth, women in their later years (fifty-five to sixty-four years) are participating more actively in the labor force than they had in years past (see Figure 7–2).[7] These increases in the number of both middle-aged and older women workers suggest some very significant changes in the roles and attitudes of women in Japanese society today.

The predominant pattern of employment among Japanese women today remains one in which young women enter the workforce after the completion of their formal education, continue to work full-time after marriage until the birth of their first child, and subsequently return to the labor force as part-time workers after their children are in school, staying there until the children complete their education (see Figure 7–2).[8] This pattern of labor force participation conforms to the so-called M-shaped curve model, with the dip in the "M" reflecting the Japanese woman's attempt to balance both her traditional role of mother and her modern role of labor force participant. It should be noted, however, that the second peak of this M-shaped curve represents primarily part-time women workers engaged in menial jobs who remain financially dependent on their husbands. While the increased rate of labor force participation among middle-aged Japanese women may suggest an improved consciousness about women's roles in modern society, the majority of these women remain within their traditional roles.

Of course, the increased participation of Japanese women in the labor force may be due more to economic necessity than awakened social consciousness, especially during the recent period of economic recession. Educating Japanese children has become a very expensive proposition, and many wives may be forced to work in order to earn additional family income. Since Japan's technological advances have obviated the need for housewives to spend all of their time on homemaking, many are able to reenter the labor force, especially once their children are in school.

International comparisons of female labor force participation rates by age reveal that while Japan is comparable to other advanced nations in terms of overall rates, Japanese rates differ significantly with respect to working women between the ages of fifteen and nineteen, and working women sixty-five years and older. With the exception of France, approximately half of the female population between the ages of fifteen and nineteen in Western industrialized societies is in the workforce today.[9] And a significantly higher proportion of Japanese and Korean women stay in the labor force past sixty-five years of age: 17 percent for Japanese, 19 percent for Koreans, and less than 5 percent for other Western societies and China. This latter fact may indicate a loss of status within the family of Japanese elderly women. In the traditional family system, older women enjoyed a respected, seniority status over the younger women in the household. Today, however, loss of economic resources may have deprived elderly women of this respect, especially in Japan and Korea but certainly less so in China.

MARITAL STATUS

The fact that an increasing number of middle-aged Japanese women participate in the labor force indicates a change in the marital status of working women. Traditionally, Japanese women worked for several years prior to marriage and then left the workforce to become full-time housewives. Thus, the majority of Japanese women in the labor force were single. Today, however, the majority of working women are married (57.6 percent), and their average age has increased as much as 10 years, from 26.3 years in 1960 to 36.0 years in 1992.[10]

LENGTH OF LABOR FORCE PARTICIPATION

Over the years, the length of full-time participation in the labor force of Japanese working women has increased significantly: from 4.0 years in 1960 to 7.4 years in 1992.[11] But their length of service is still much shorter than that of their male counterparts (12.5 years in 1992) because women must also fulfill their traditional roles of housewife and mother. Women's shorter term of service in the workforce relative to men's results in a significantly lower level of monetary remuneration. Although the gap has been narrowing over the years, in 1992 the average monthly salary for a full-time female worker was only 61.5 percent of the average male salary (it was only 45.0 percent in 1960.)[12]

EMPLOYMENT STRUCTURE

Despite legal guarantees ensuring equal employment opportunity for women, their entry into professions and managerial positions remains quite discouraging. Similar to women in other industrialized societies, the majority of Japanese working women today still hold low-skilled jobs. In 1992, 34.9 percent of working women were engaged in clerical work, 19.5 percent in manufacturing, and 11.2 percent in service sectors, totaling 65.6 percent. This represents little improvement over the 71.2 percent of working women holding such jobs in 1970. Consequently, there has been only a marginal increase in the number of women in professional positions: 13.7 percent in 1992 versus 9.1 percent in 1975. Of all working women in 1992, only 1.0 percent held managerial positions (versus 0.5 percent in 1970),[13] this despite the equal opportunity legislation that guarantees equality of employment regardless of gender.

PART-TIME WORKERS

Another significant trend among Japanese working women is the increasing number who work part-time (i.e., less than thirty-five hours per week). The proportion of part-time women workers has been rising steadily from 8.9 percent (570,000 workers) in 1960 to 30.7 percent (5.92 million workers) in 1992.[14] In 1992, of all part-time workers in Japan (8.68 million), 68.2 percent were women.

Part-time women workers in Japan typically work six hours per day, 20.9 days per month.[15] A great majority of them (88.1 percent) are paid by the hour at an average hourly wage of ¥809.[16] They tend to work for small-size organizations in the retail, wholesale, or food industries (34.6 percent), the service industry (29.1 percent), or the manufacturing industry (21.3 percent).[17] More than eight in every ten of these women are thirty-five years of age or older and thus most likely to be those who have completed their child-rearing roles.[18]

In fact, a great majority of these part-time workers are married (80.6 percent) with an average of 1.8 children (54.9 percent). Of this group, a predominantly large number have completed their principal child-rearing roles (school-age children: 82.3 percent; preschool-age children: 9.5 percent; both preschool- and school-age children: 8.2 percent).[19] With less time required for child-rearing responsibilities at home, Japanese housewives today participate actively in the workforce, although primarily in the form of part-time supplementary and temporary work. Part-time women workers appear to work for the same reasons as full-time women workers: to earn extra income for themselves and for their families. For married women who work part-time, achieving economic independence and realizing one's own potential are not really major reasons for work.[20]

EQUAL OPPORTUNITY FOR EMPLOYMENT

Although equal opportunity for women and men in the workplace has yet to be fully achieved, the enactment of the Equal Opportunity Law (EOL) in April 1986 has led to significant progress in Japanese employment practices. Now female college graduates may choose between *sogo-shoku* (comprehensive career-track positions), in which work conditions are identical to those of their male counterparts, or *ippan-shoku* (general clerical positions), in which only women are assigned. The percentage of job offers made to new college graduates regardless of sex increased from 32.4 percent in 1986 to 72.0 percent in 1987, a year after the enactment of the EOL,[21] although certain types of jobs (i.e., engineering/ science positions) are still offered predominantly to male college graduates.[22]

The impact of a lingering economic recession in Japan since the summer of 1991, however, has had a deleterious effect on the opportunities for women college graduates. In fact, the proportion of job offers made to new college graduates regardless of sex has declined by 20 percent over the past five-year period (51.5 percent in 1992).[23] Despite signs of a gradual recovery for the Japanese economy, the time lags involved for this recovery to impact the job market ensure that the traditional practice of women being the last hired and the first fired will continue.

In 1988 the Ministry of Labor recommended that each organization appoint an affirmative action officer to monitor how closely the organization's conduct accords with the objectives of the EOL. As of September 1989, there were approximately 28,000 affirmative action officers throughout Japan, most of whom were male personnel managers belonging to organizations with more than thirty employees.[24] The Ministry of Labor aims to increase this number to 50,000 by 1993. It is somewhat ironic that the EOL offers no stipulations regarding punishment for those organizations that do not follow EOL regulations. Under these circumstances, enforcement of equal opportunity in Japan is difficult to achieve, no matter how many affirmative action officers may be appointed.

Unfortunately, most affirmative action officers have been appointed to large organizations in urban areas, which are more likely to observe equal opportunity legislation than small-scale, regional organizations. In fact, since the passage of the EOL, the number of female college graduates employed by large-scale organizations with 1,000 or more employees increased from 36.4 percent in 1985 to 50 percent in 1989. But, perhaps due to the economic recession, this number declined again to 41.1 percent in 1992.[25] It is in rural areas where employment continues to be defined by traditional sex role allocations.

Of course, one of the truest tests of equal employment opportunity arises during periods of recession when there are limited job opportunities for both women and men. Following the recent burst of Japan's bubble economy in the early 1990s, many female college seniors were told by firms that there were no plans to hire women college students in the near future. Although in clear violation of the EOL, some companies publicly announced that they would recruit only male college students for comprehensive career-track positions and female high school seniors or junior college students for general clerical positions.[26] Again, these blatantly discriminatory practices can go unchecked since there is no provision in the EOL to penalize companies for failing to accord with its provisions.

Results of a study on the attitudes of Japanese women holding comprehensive career-track positions have been recently made public by the Ministry of Labor.[27] This study is the first of its kind to reveal the real situation confronted by Japanese *sogo-shoku* women. Six important characteristics emerged.

First, nearly eight out of ten (77.0 percent) of these women felt that their abilities and skills were actively utilized in their current workplaces. Second, job satisfaction was found to be quite high: two thirds (62.5 percent) were completely satisfied with their work, with a direct correlation emerging between length of work and the level of their job satisfaction. Third, seven out of ten young women today see their jobs as long-term career pursuits, rather than temporary work opportunities. More than one third (37.0 percent) planned to continue their careers, while another one third (37.5) wished to continue working after marriage and childbearing as long as systems and facilities were in place to enable them to fulfill both their workplace and family responsibilities. Fourth, a substantially large proportion (60.1 percent) reported sex discrimination in the workplace, particularly with regard to recruitment and hiring, promotion, assignment, and job training. To alleviate these problems, seven out of ten of the victims expressed a concern that understanding and appreciation of fellow women workers must be enhanced among male superiors and colleagues. Fifth, although only one out of ten (9.9 percent) of these women workers experienced job assignment transfers entailing geographical relocation, as many as 60 percent expressed a willingness to accept a job relocation if their duties required it. Finally, more than four out of ten (40.5 percent) believed that regulations concerning women working late in the evening should be removed. They felt that women should work on an equal footing with their male counterparts, regardless of their additional domestic responsibilities.

These results reveal very positive attitudes among young working women who pursue comprehensive career-track positions in Japan today. Nevertheless, it is clear that these highly talented and aspiring women continue to face unwarranted sexual discrimination in the workplace, and equal opportunity for women will never be fully realized until Japanese men accept the fact that women are their equals. Perhaps in recognition of this, Keizai Doyukai (Japanese Federation of Business Leaders) has recently published a sixty-four-page *manga* book that purports to make the workplace more comfortable for Japanese women. Hopefully, this type of effort will contribute to enhancing a social consciousness of equality among both men and women in Japanese society.[28]

WOMEN HOLDING MANAGERIAL/EXECUTIVE POSITIONS

Women in management are still a minority in Japan. Although the proportion of women managers in Japanese companies has increased from 2.5 percent in 1960 to 7.4 percent in 1992,[29] the majority of these women are in the lower echelons of management and have no support staff to supervise.[30] This figure is substantially lower than that of their American counterparts, who account for 42.4 percent of the total managerial personnel in U.S. corporations.[31] Given that Japanese women in managerial positions constitute only 1 percent of the total female workforce in Japan today, compared to 11.1 percent in the United States,[32] it is evident that Japanese career women still have a long way to go in order to break through the glass ceiling.

To aid this effort, some companies have started providing special seminars exclusively for women to prepare them for managerial positions.[33] More and more women (some 61 percent) are also relying on female mentors to inspire confidence in themselves and to better prepare for promotional opportunities.[34]

THE FUTURE OF JAPANESE WOMEN

Since the enactment of the EOL in 1986, significant progress has been made toward achieving equality of the sexes in the workplace. But legal channels for equal employment opportunity notwithstanding, Japanese women continue to place a higher value on their domestic responsibilities than on the pursuit of careers. Clearly, social support structures that enable women to pursue careers while at the same time fulfilling their family responsibilities will play a crucial role in leveling the playing field for women and men in the Japanese workplace.

Of course, the primary prerequisite for equality between men and women must begin with women themselves. As long as women choose to take the easy road in the workplace, they will never be accepted as genuine partners by their male colleagues. It is imperative, therefore, that Japanese women continue to aspire to the highest levels, or the liberalization of the female sex in Japan will never be attained.

With the passage of the Maternity Leave Law in April 1992, married women workers in Japan have begun to request employers to develop systematic welfare programs that permit leaves of absence to nurse children, enforce five-day workweeks, increase the number of holiday and vacation days, or allow for flex-time. In this way, women workers can better balance their work and family responsibilities and support a work-sharing system. Similar support structures will also be needed to support women workers as they endeavor to pursue their careers while caring for the increasing number of the nation's elderly population.

NOTES

1. Women's Bureau of the Ministry of Labor, 1993b, supplementary table.
2. Ibid.
3. The Japanese Ministry of Labor classifies industry into three types: primary industry (farming, forestry, and fishery); secondary industry (mining, constructions, and manufacturing); and tertiary industry (all other types). Changes over time in female labor force participation rates (LFPRs) by industry are shown below. Statistical Bureau of the Prime Minister's Office, 1920–1975; idem, 1980–1988; Women's Bureau of the Ministry of Labor, 1993b, supplementary table.

Year	Female Total LFPR	Female Primary Industry	Female Secondary Industry	Female Tertiary Industry
1920	53.4	62.4	16.3	19.4
1930	49.1	60.9	14.1	24.9
1940	52.6	57.2	15.6	26.7
1950	48.6	61.2	13.2	25.5

1955	50.6	52.2	16.7	31.1
1960	54.5	43.1	20.2	36.7
1965	50.6	32.5	23.1	44.4
1970	49.9	26.2	26.0	47.8
1975	45.7	18.4	25.7	55.7
1980	47.6	13.2	28.2	58.4
1985	48.7	10.6	28.3	60.8
1990	50.1	8.5	27.3	63.8
1992	50.7	7.3	27.1	65.1

4. Ministry of Education, Basic Survey of Education, reported in Women's Bureau of the Ministry of Labor, 1992, supplementary table 39; Ministry of Education, 1993a, 6, tables 9 and 10.

5. Institute of Population Problems, 1990, 84, table 9–2; Women's Bureau of the Ministry of Labor, 1993b, supplementary table 2.

6. Institute of Population Problems, 1993: 22, Table 2–2; Women's Bureau of the Ministry of Labor, 1993b, supplementary table 2.

7. Women's Bureau of the Ministry of Labor, 1993b, supplementary table 2.

8. Ibid.

9. Institute of Population Problems, 1993a, 103–104, tables 8–3, 8–4.

10. Women's Bureau of the Ministry of Labor, 1993b, supplementary tables 15 and 21. Changes over time in the proportion of working single women versus married women are as follows (statistics exclude women in farming and forestry industries): 1962: 55.2 percent versus 32.7 percent; 1970: 48.3 percent versus 41.4 percent; 1975: 38.0 percent versus 51.3 percent; 1985: 31.3 percent versus 59.2 percent; 1990: 32.7 percent versus 58.2 percent; 1992: 33.1 percent versus 57.6 percent. From supplementary table 11.

11. Ibid., supplementary table 21.

12. Ibid., supplementary table 42.

13. Ibid., supplementary table 11.

14. Ibid., supplementary table 66.

15. Ibid., supplementary table 70.

16. Ibid., supplementary tables 71 and 76.

17. Ibid., supplementary table 67.

18. Ibid., supplementary table 41.

19. Ibid.

20. Life Insurance Cultural Center, 1992, 58–59.

21. 1987 report of Josei Shokugyo Zaidan, reported in Women's Bureau of the Ministry of Labor, 1990, 49.

22. Ibid., 78.

23. Women's Bureau of the Ministry of Labor, 1993b, 26, table 1–3.

24. *Japan Economic Journal*, 1990e.

25. Women's Bureau of the Ministry of Labor, 1990, supplementary table 79; and idem, 1993b, supplementary table 20.

26. *Japan Economic Journal*, 1993e, 25. Women's Bureau of the Ministry of Labor, 1992, appendix 21.

27. Ministry of Labor, 1994. Questionnaires were sent to relevant women workers at 360 corporations during the months of September and October 1993. Of the total 744 responses obtained, 70 percent were from women less than thirty years of age, with approximately fifty-fifty proportions of less than five years and more than five years of experience.

28. Keizai Doyukai, 1994. This booklet will be distributed by the federation to concerned companies and individuals.

29. Women's Bureau of the Ministry of Labor, 1992, supplementary table 24.

30. Ibid., supplementary table 25.

31. Ibid., supplementary table 95.

32. Ibid., appendices 11 and 95.

33. *Japan Economic Journal*, 1993c.

34. *Japan Economic Journal*, 1993g.

PART IV

THE GRAYING OF JAPAN

CHAPTER 8

Aging as a Sociocultural Process

Aging is more than a biological process; it is a sociocultural process as well. Social and cultural conditions have a significant impact not only on how rapidly we age but on what aging means to us and how we respond to it. Although the issue of aging is an international phenomenon, the graying of Japan is unique in several respects: One is the rate at which the change is progressing, and the other is the important effect that it is having on Japanese society and culture.[1]

As is true for most modern industrialized societies, the aging of the population poses serious problems. But the Japanese situation is again complicated by the coexistence of modernity and tradition within a single social structure.

In principle, Japanese people accord a significant degree of respect to the elderly. In Japan's "seniority-based society," the majority of high-ranking positions in government and business and professional organizations are held by "honorable elders." Stemming from the Confucian precept of filial piety, the Japanese government has proclaimed September 15 "Respect for the Aged Day," a national holiday celebrated each year.

In reality, however, the majority of Japanese elderly are welcomed neither by society nor by the family. Due to their relative loss of economic power, many elderly Japanese find themselves in inferior positions and are frequently subject to psychological pressure by younger generations.

Japan's elderly have experienced drastic political, economic, and social change throughout their lifetime. In a single century, they have experienced the transition from an old imperial order to a modernized form of government and society, and from total devastation in war to an unprecedented rate of economic and technological development. Together they have come to appreciate the significance of hard work, not for themselves but for the sake of their country. Thus, it is an extremely difficult task for the elderly in Japan to adjust to the dependency that old age inevitably brings.

THE DEMOGRAPHICS OF AGING IN JAPAN

Approximately one in every eight Japanese is sixty-five years and older today, one of the lowest proportions of the industrial nations (see Figure 8–1).[2] Nevertheless, it will take as few as twenty-five years for the proportion of the elderly population in Japan to double from 7 to 14 percent (1970–1995), while it has taken a much longer period for most Western industrial nations.[3]

Furthermore, the proportion of elderly in Japan is projected to constitute 17.03 percent of the total population by the year 2000 and will be the world's highest (27.28 percent) by the year 2020 (see Figure 8–2).[4] In absolute numbers, the Japanese elderly population is expected to increase from 14.93 to 32.74 million between 1990 (12.08 percent of the total population) and 2020 (25.51 percent of the total population),[5] or to more than double in just over three decades. No other nation in the world has ever undergone such an extremely rapid aging process.

FACTORS CONTRIBUTING TO AGING IN JAPAN

Three significant trends in Japanese society have produced the graying of Japan: a sharply declining birth rate, two generations of baby boomers, and a prolonged life expectancy among Japanese people.

Figure 8–1
Changes in the Proportion of the Elderly Sixty-Five and Over in Five Countries: 1900–2025

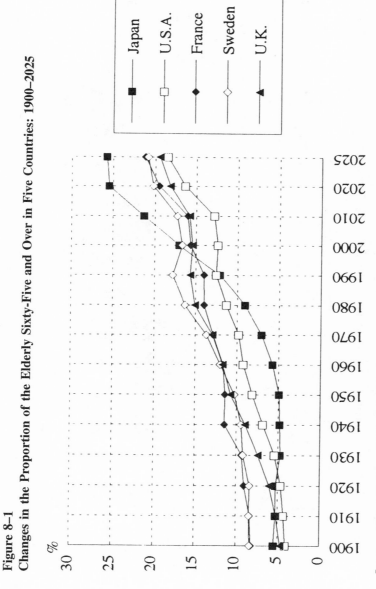

Sources: United Nations, 1956, United Nations, *World Population Prospects: 1988,* reported in the Institute of Population Problems, Ministry of Health and Welfare, 1990, 40, table 3–14.

Figure 8–2
Changes in Percent Distributions of the Japanese Population by Three Age Groups: 1884–2020

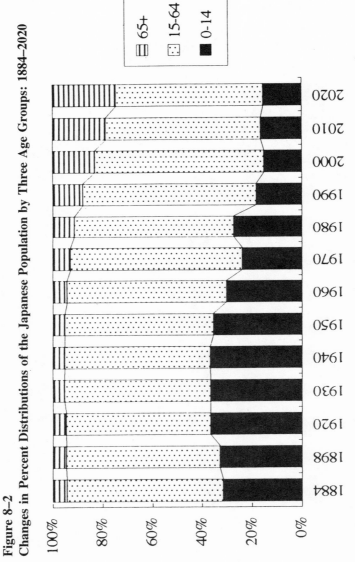

Source: Institute of Population Problems, Ministry of Health and Welfare, 1993a, 27, tables 2–5 and 2–7.

Declining Birth Rates

In the postwar period, the total fertility rate among Japanese women has undergone dramatic change:[6] As high as 5.11 in 1925, it declined to as low as 1.50 in 1992.[7] Already at an alarming level well below that required to sustain the nation's population, this low fertility rate is expected to continue into the future. A small family orientation has come to be well established among the Japanese people due to the high cost of housing and children's education and the increased employment of women.[8] Also, the majority of young people, women especially, consider some period of "single life" before marriage to be desirable. These trends have led to a much larger proportion of elderly to young people in Japanese society.

Baby Boomer Generations

The impact of two Japanese baby boomer populations (8.06 million born between 1947 and 1949, and 8.16 million born between 1971 and 1974) has also contributed to the rapid rate of aging in Japan. By the time all the people in the first baby boomer generation are launched into old age, the proportion of the Japanese elderly will exceed one in every five people.[9]

Increased Life Expectancy

Japanese people today are also living longer than ever before (see Figure 8–3.) The life expectancy at birth of both Japanese men and women is now the highest in the world: 78.09 years for men and 82.22 years for women.[10] The "longevity revolution" experienced by most industrialized societies during the twentieth century has been most pronounced in Japan, where the increase in life expectancy has been both more rapid and more extensive than that of any other country. According to recent projections, the high level of life expectancy among Japanese men and women is expected to be the highest in the world throughout the twenty-first century.

The rising life expectancy in Japan has also resulted in the aging of the elderly population itself. While the elderly seventy-five years and

Figure 8–3

Changes and Projections of Life Expectancy at Birth of Japanese Male and Female: 1920–2025

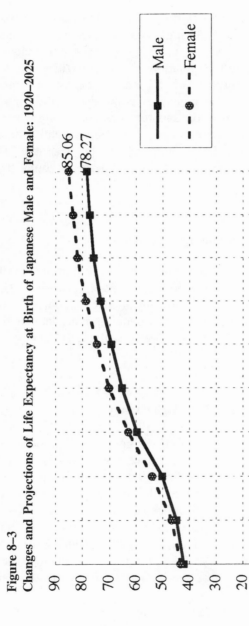

Sources: Institute of Population Problems, Ministry of Health and Welfare, 1993a, 58, table 5–10; Ministry of Health and Welfare, 1993.

older constituted only one quarter of the total elderly population in 1920, this proportion has increased to four out of ten today (39.8 percent in 1992) and is projected to rise as high as 56.2 percent by 2025.[11] In the twenty-first century, the population of the older elderly will exceed more than half of the total elderly population (see Figure 8–4).

The age structure of the elderly population also differs by sex. Historically, the proportion of younger elderly men has been greater than that of younger elderly women, and this difference has increased over time. The older elderly, however, are overrepresented by women. In 1993, for example, the proportion of men per 100 women was 68.9 for the sixty-five to sixty-nine years age group, 57.4 for the seventy-five to seventy-nine years age group, and as low as 44.7 for the eighty-five years and over age group[12]. Thus, even though more elderly men are living longer than ever before, there are still more elderly women in Japan who are, on the average, older than their elderly male counterparts. Of the population sixty-five years and older, there were 1.29 million more women in 1993,[13] and by the year 2025, this gap is expected to expand to as many as 4.63 million.[14] Consequently, the problems inherent in the aging process can be expected to be felt most severely by Japanese women.

MARITAL STATUS OF JAPAN'S AGED

The marital status of Japanese elderly differs significantly by sex and age. The proportion of married elderly men is much higher than that of married elderly women: 90 percent of men in their sixties are married, as are 80 percent of men in their seventies and more than half eighty-five years and older. However, of all women in their late seventies, less than 30 percent are married. Although widowhood increases substantially with age for both men and women, the majority of Japanese women continue to outlive their husbands for two major reasons: In the early twentieth century, the average life expectancy of women was two to three years longer than men, and most elderly women were about four years younger than their husbands at first marriage.[15] In consequence, the average Japanese woman must expect to be a widow for approximately six to seven years.

Rates of Japanese married elderly have been increasing over time for both men and women across different age groups. This does not mean, however, that Japanese elderly remain in their first marriages. Elderly

Figure 8–4
Changes in the Proportion of the Japanese Elderly by Age Group: 1930–2025

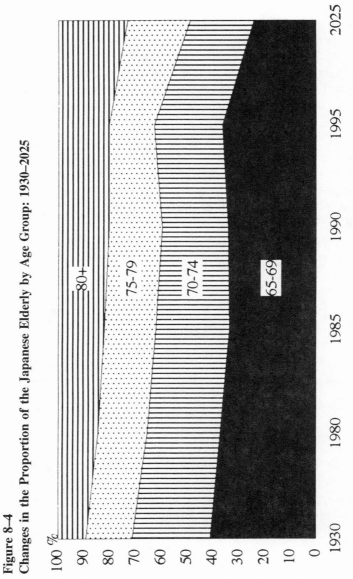

Sources: Institute of Population Problems, Ministry of Health and Welfare, 1933a, 22–23, tables 2–2 and 2–3; and calculations were made by the author.

men are much more likely to remarry than women due to the availability of eligible partners. At the same time, the traditional orientation of Japanese culture continues to prevent widows from actively seeking remarriage. Widowhood is considered indicative of a woman's loyalty to her deceased husband and is still regarded as a virtue of Japanese womanhood.

Enjoying life after retirement as a couple is not yet a lifestyle fully appreciated by Japanese. Most Japanese men who have devoted their lives to working outside the home find it difficult to manage free time after their retirement. And by the time their husbands retire from work, most Japanese women have established independent lifestyles that do not include their husbands. The unaccustomed full-time presence of husbands at home often has a negative impact on family life. Thus, Japanese wives often refer to their unwelcome retired husbands as *sodaigomi* (large useless trash) or *nure ochiba* (wet leaves that stick around even after sweeping). Marital stress, difficult to cope with under the best of circumstances, becomes even more so for the elderly, particularly if their health and economic conditions are deteriorating.

HEALTH AND ADJUSTMENT TO THE AGING PROCESS

Health is generally recognized to be one of the major factors in determining an elderly person's satisfaction with life. Therefore, it is somewhat surprising to find that the majority of Japanese elderly feel that they are healthy (75.4 percent of elderly men and 72.7 percent of elderly women).[16]

Each year on or near September 15, Japan's national holiday in honor of the elderly, the Ministry of Health and Welfare publishes a list of the very old elderly who will reach 100 years of age or more by the end of that September. In 1993, the list included 4,802 people (men: 943 [19.6 percent]; women: 3,859 [80.4 percent]), an increase of 650 people from the previous year. These very old elderly constituted 0.03 percent of the total elderly population 65 years and older (16,900,000; men: 0.01 percent of 6,893,000; women: 0.04 percent of 10,007,000).[17] Although still an extremely small proportion of the total number of elderly people in Japan today, the increase in the number of these very old people has been extremely rapid. Two decades ago when this survey was first conducted, there were only 153 people 100 years and older in Japan. Their number exceeded 1,000 by 1981, 2,000 by 1987, and 4,000 by 1992.

These very old elderly live most frequently in the western part of Japan. In comparison with the national average of 3.86 in 1993, the proportion of the elderly 100 years and over per 100,000 population was the highest in Okinawa (16.64), followed by Shimane (10.71), Kochi (9.91), Kagoshima (8.17), and Kumamoto (7.53). Prefectures with the lowest proportions of very old elderly were Saitama (1.46), Akita (1.89), Osaka (1.96), Chiba (2.31), and Aichi (2.45). This unbalanced geographical representation coincides with the general tendency of elderly Japanese—popularly called *seiko-totei* (or high in the West and low in the East)—to reside in the western rather than the eastern part of Japan.

According to a survey of people 100 years and older conducted in the spring of 1993,[18] there are two secrets to living a long life: maintaining a worry-free, relaxed attitude toward life, and eating only until one is eight-tenths full. Of those surveyed, nearly half continued to lead healthy and independent lives without the assistance of daily care providers. Most (66 percent) continued to reside at home; only one fifth were living in nursing homes, and slightly more than one tenth (12 percent) were hospitalized. In the case of men, however, nearly eight out of ten (79 percent) were living at home.

When Japanese men and women between thirty and sixty years of age were asked what concerned them most about growing old, the most common concern was their health, followed by happy marital relations, good family relations, economic stability, hobbies and work, and friends.[19] When asked who they would like to be their primary care provider, should they become frail or bed-ridden, more than half of the respondents named their spouses (52.1 percent), followed by daughters (13.8 percent), institutions (9.0 percent), daughters-in-law (6.9 percent), sons (3.7 percent), and children (3.5 percent).[20]

A recent study of the lifestyles and attitudes of the elderly in Japan, Korea, the United States, England, and Germany revealed that the desire for a primary care provider differs between Asian and Western societies.[21] Whereas the elderly in both Japan and Korea seek their primary care providers from among close relatives, such as spouses and coresiding and nonresiding children, those in Western societies extend this circle to include more distant relatives as well as friends and acquaintances.

Preferences among Japanese people for primary care providers differ by sex and age of respondents (see Figures 8–5a and 8–5b). While the majority of men (75.0 percent) want to be taken care of by their spouses, only one third of the women (33.6 percent) desire their spouses to be

Figure 8–5
The Proportion of Care Providers by Whom One Desires to Be Taken Care of When Becoming Old and Frail by Sex and Age Group

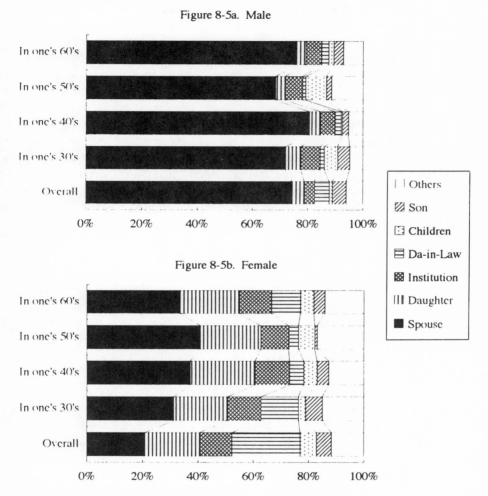

Figure 8-5a. Male

Figure 8-5b. Female

Source: Management and Coordination Agency, 1990, 35, table 31.

care providers. Women prefer daughters-in-law to their spouses, as is expected in the traditional stem family, and relatively high proportions of women across all age groups (21.4 percent) expressed a desire that their own daughters become caregivers. Twice as many women as men (11.6 percent versus 5.7 percent) would prefer to enter nursing homes, should they become physically infirm.[22]

SUICIDE AMONG THE ELDERLY

The suicide rate in Japan increases with age, and for the most part, males are more than twice as likely to commit suicide as females. The exception to this rule can be found among the elderly population in Japan: The suicide rate for elderly women is much higher than for elderly men, suggesting the extreme difficulties women must face in their old age.

Older people's life satisfaction is likely to depend on their ability to adjust to and cope with changes in the life cycle. Failure to adjust to aging leads to depression, which in turn results in a high rate of suicide among the elderly. In 1992 the overall suicide rate in Japan was eighth highest in the world: 17.8 per 10,000 people. However, the rate for elderly Japanese between the ages of sixty-five and seventy-four was 34.1 (sixth highest in the world), and for those seventy-five years and over, it was 61.4 (third highest in the world after Hungary and Austria). Furthermore, the suicide rate of Japanese women seventy-five years and older was 54.9, second highest in the world.[23]

Of all suicides in Japan in 1992, nearly three out of ten (27.0 percent) were committed by the elderly sixty-five years and over. Major reasons for these suicide cases were health problems (more than 40 percent) and financial problems (nearly 10 percent). In addition, there are increasing numbers of double suicides among elderly couples who live by themselves, especially when elderly wives become ill and elderly husbands serve as the primary care providers.

But suicide among the elderly occurs not only because of ill health. In some regions in Japan, elderly people still commit suicide because they feel themselves to be a burden on their families. Although the age-old tradition of carrying elderly, burdensome women into the mountains to die may no longer be practiced, suicide is still regarded by some as a natural life course. In fact, one county in Niigata prefecture is called Kubiki county—*kubiki* means hanging by one's neck.

REGIONAL VARIATIONS IN AGING

According to 1992 population estimates by the Statistics Bureau of the Management and Coordination Agency, the proportions of elderly in Japan vary significantly by region. Among Japan's forty-seven prefectures, the highest proportion of elderly (19.7 percent) was found in Shimane, followed by Kochi (18.6 percent) and Kagoshima (17.9 percent). Prefectures with relatively low proportions of elderly were Saitama (9.0 percent), Kanagawa (9.7 percent), Chiba (10.0 percent), and satellite prefectures of the Tokyo metropolis (11.5 percent).[24] By the year 2000, however, population projections reveal that the process of aging in Japanese society will accelerate evenly across both depopulated rural areas and highly populated urban regions.[25]

Primary Care Providers

A great majority (89.6 percent) of primary care providers for the frail elderly are women. Of these women, 37.0 percent are daughters-in-law; 24.7 percent, elderly wives; and 17.8 percent, daughters.[26] Reflecting the traditional nature of family relations in Japan's rural areas, daughters-in-law still continue to serve as primary care providers. Secondary care providers in rural areas are sons (50.0 percent) or wives of grandsons (50.0 percent). In urban Tokyo, on the other hand, primary care providers are not only daughters-in-law (57.14 percent) but also daughters (21.43 percent) and spouses (7.14 percent).[27] Secondary care providers are most frequently daughters (25.0 percent), followed by various others both in and outside the family. This, perhaps, is indicative of the more complex family structure in urban settings.

Senile Dementia

Although exact figures are difficult to obtain, it is generally believed that approximately 5 percent of the Japanese elderly sixty-five years and older experience some form of senile dementia.[28] The rate of occurrence, however, varies significantly by region and age. In urban Tokyo, the occurrence rate increases from 2 percent for those between sixty-five and sixty-nine years, to 14 percent for those between eighty and eighty-four years, and to 27 percent for those eighty-five years and older. For elderly in rural areas, however, the occurrence rate of senile dementia is significantly higher: More than half of the very old are likely to suffer from senile dementia.[29] While the reasons for this regional variation are no doubt complex, one contributing factor may be the lack of active stimuli for the elderly living in remote rural regions.

There are two primary causes of senile dementia: cerebral hemorrhage and degenerative brain disease, commonly known as Alzheimer's disease. Effective treatments have yet to be established for either of these two types. Of the total Japanese elderly population (16,870,000 in 1993), approximately 1 million (5.9 percent) are currently suffering from senile dementia, and 30 to 50 percent of these cases are of the Alzheimer's type.

Given the acute aging of Japanese society, increases in the number of senile dementia cases must be expected. In fact, the Ministry of Health and Welfare estimates that the number of elderly who suffer from senile dementia will increase to 1.5 million by the year 2000 (6.9 percent of a total elderly population of 21,699,000) and to as many as 2.13 million by the year 2010 (7.7 percent of 27,746,000 elderly persons sixty-five years and older).[30] Although various short-stay and day-care services for those suffering from senile dementia are currently available, more comprehensive public support programs and services will most certainly be required in the foreseeable future.

NOTES

1. Kumagai, 1987a, 225.

2. Some 13.5 percent as of September 15, 1993, according to the Management and Coordination Agency. Proportions of the elderly sixty-five years and older in other Western societies in 1990 were as follows: United States, 12.6 percent; Sweden, 17.8 percent; United Kingdom, 15.7 percent; Italy, 14.1 percent; France, 13.9 percent; Germany, 14.6 percent; and Switzerland, 15.1 percent. United Nations, *The Sex and Age Distribution of World Populations: 1992*, reported in the Institute of Population Problems, 1993a, 33, table 2–16.

3. Years taken to double the elderly population 65 years and older from 7 to 14 percent in six Western industrial nations are as follows: France, 130 years (1865–1995); Sweden, 85 years (1890–1975); United States, 70 years (1945–2015); United Kingdom, 50 years (1930–1980); Switzerland, 50 years (1935–1985); and Germany, 45 years (1930–1975). United Nations, 1956; United Nations, *The Sex and Age Distribution of World Populations: 1992*, reported in the Institute of Population Problems, 1993a, 33, table 2–16; Institute of Population Problems, 1993a, 34, table 2–17.

4. Institute of Population Problems, 1993a, Nihon University Population Research Institute, 1993.

5. Institute of Population Problems, 1993a, 27, table 2–6.

6. The total fertility rate is the average number of children born to a woman

in her productive years, assuming she expects to give birth. Changes over time in the total fertility rate of Japanese women are as follows: 1925: 5.1; 1930: 4.7; 1940: 4.1; 1950: 3.7; 1960: 2.0; 1970: 2.1; 1980: 1.75; 1989: 1.57. Institute of Population Problems, 1990, 48, table 5–5; Statistical Bureau of the Ministry of Health and Welfare, 1990a, 2, table 2.

7. Kumagai, 1990c; Institute of Population Problems, 1992, 34, table 3–4; Statistical Bureau of the Ministry of Health and Welfare, 1993a.

8. Kuroda, 1988.

9. Kumagai, 1990.

10. Ministry of Health and Welfare, 1993a.

11. Calculated from the Institute of Population Problems, 1993a, 22–23, tables 2–2 and 2–3.

12. Statistical Bureau of the Prime Minister's Office, 1993, 1, table 1.

13. Ibid.

14. Calculated from the Institute of Population Problems, 1993a, 23, table 2–3.

15. Ibid., 57, table 5–9; 75, table 6–12; 82, table 6–23.

16. Statistical Bureau of the Ministry of Health and Welfare, 1990c, 24.

17. Ministry of Health and Welfare, 1993. A compilation of the elderly who would be 100 years and older by the end of September as of September 1, 1993.

18. Ministry of Health and Welfare, 1993b. With the assistance of affiliated prefectural and community organizations throughout Japan, the Ministry of Health and Welfare conducted survey interviews of all elderly 100 years and older in the spring (March-May) of 1993. A total of 2,851 elderly (men: 548; women: 2303) were interviewed.

19. Prime Minister's Office, 1990b, 28.

20. Ibid., 34–35, table 31.

21. Office of Aging, Prime Minister's Office, 1991, 9–10. Interviews were conducted with men and women sixty years and older in these five countries in November and December 1990. Slightly more than 1,000 people in each country took part in the interviews.

22. Prime Minister's Office, 1990b, 34–35, table 31.

23. Police Agency, 1990, 1993.

24. Institute of Population Problems, 1989, 105, table 167, idem, 1992, 135, table 12–11; Statistics Bureau of the Management and Coordination Agency, 1993, 64–65, table 17.

25. Statistics Bureau of the Management and Coordination Agency, 1993, 25, table 4–3.

26. Economic Planning Agency, 1986, 102–103.

27. Kumagai, 1987b, 32–33.

28. Hasegawa, 1987.

29. Ibid., 78.

30. Institute of Population Problems, 1993a, 27, table 2–6; Ministry of Health and Welfare, Committee for the Study of Senile Dementia, 1993, reported in *Japan Economic Journal*, 1993j; Statistical Bureau of the Prime Minister's Office, 1993, 1, table 1.

CHAPTER 9

The Economics of Aging

The graying of Japan has significant implications not only for the Japanese family and society, but also for the Japanese economy.

LABOR FORCE PARTICIPATION

One of the most outstanding characteristics of the Japanese elderly is their comparatively high rate of participation in the labor force, a pattern that holds true for both sexes. Even though these rates have been declining over time, one third of the men (38.2 percent) and one in every six of the women (16.7 percent) aged sixty-five years were in the labor force in 1992.[1] This represents a tripling of elderly workers in the labor force over the past quarter century.[2]

Compared with other industrialized nations in the world, the high rate of labor force participation of the elderly in Japan is particularly outstanding. This is especially true for Japanese elderly men between sixty and sixty-four years of age and for both sexes sixty-five years and over. In 1991, slightly more than seven out of every ten Japanese elderly men between sixty and sixty-four years of age (76.1 percent) were in the labor force, compared to between three and five of every ten elderly men in the United States (55.1 percent), Germany (35.1 percent), and France (18.7 percent).[3]

The rapid aging of the Japanese people, along with their desire to work into old age, has prompted this increase in elderly workers. Seven in every ten Japanese males sixty years and older (69.6 percent) consider the desirable age for retirement to be at least sixty-five years (versus 51.7 percent in the United States; 46.3 percent in Korea; 39.3 percent in Germany; and 29.7 percent in the United Kingdom), while one third of Japanese females sixty years and older (34.8 percent) wish to work into their old age (versus 34.9 percent in the United States, 31.4 percent in Korea, 13.7 percent in the United Kingdom and 8.7 percent in Germany).[4] Although the desire to work into old age is clearly stronger among male than female adults, the majority of Japanese adults have indicated that they would like to work until they are at least sixty-five years old, and among these, 22.3 percent want to work as long as they can. In European societies such as England and Germany, however, more than half of the males and seven out of ten females sixty years and over desire to quit working.

One reason for the Japanese people's strong desire to continue working into old age is perhaps their cultural predisposition to value hard work over the enjoyment of leisure time. Studies reveal that while these values may be changing among the younger generation, a full 35 percent of Japanese people between the ages of thirty and seventy still want to work as long as possible (39 percent want to combine work and hobbies, 14 percent do not want to work, and 10 percent never thought of working).[5]

Another reason for the remarkably high rate of employment among Japanese elderly and their desire to work into old age no doubt stems from economic necessity. For Japanese men in particular, attaining economic independence in their old age is a major consideration. In fact, the majority of Japanese adults (64.3 percent) plan to support themselves in old age by working as long as possible. Only a quarter of Japanese adults (25.4 percent) plan to depend solely on public pensions, and only a fraction (7.7 percent) consider it their family's responsibility. This desire to work into old age for economic reasons is not only true for Japanese elderly, but also evident among the elderly in other societies. Of those sixty years and older, 65.0 percent in Korea, 46.8 percent in the United Kingdom, and 41.9 percent in the United States share this concern, but not so in Germany (28.6 percent) where the major incentive for working into old age is for sheer enjoyment (51.8 percent).[6]

Planned sources of income for supporting the Japanese elderly in their old age include public pensions (90.1 percent), savings and private pensions (21.4 percent), and support from relatives (3.1 percent).[7] The current pension scheme introduced in 1986 has a two-tier system: the first tier, flat-rate basic benefits covering all, including self-employed, and the second tier, earnings-related benefits applied only to employees. Employees' contributions to the pension plan are deducted from their salaries directly, and the self-employed make contributions themselves through their local government offices.

In the past, women who had not been employed and were dependent on their husbands' incomes were sometimes disadvantaged in the case of divorce or disability since they were not eligible to receive old-age pension benefits. However, with the introduction of the two-tier system, every woman is eligible for basic pension benefits, and her contribution is deducted from her husband's salary.

As an additional means to ensure a stable life for the elderly, a system was introduced whereby no tax is chargeable on the interest on postal savings of widowed women and people over sixty years of age. The Ministry of Post and Telecommunications also offers schemes combining life insurance and pension insurance for couples. After deregulation of private insurance, a greater number of life insurance and pension schemes have become available.[8]

Nevertheless, pensions, social security, and other retirement benefits that the elderly receive are generally recognized to be insufficient for them to live on. For widows who have never held a full-time job and therefore are not qualified to receive any retirement pension except that received indirectly from their spouses, it is almost impossible to maintain an independent household. Therefore, many Japanese elderly widows are forced to adopt coresidency living arrangements.

RETIREMENT

Since the mid-1970s, most Japanese firms have adopted a uniform retirement age system. According to the Ministry of Labor's 1988 *Survey on Employment Management*, 88.3 percent of all Japanese firms had such a system: 99 percent for firms with 300 and more employees, 97.2 percent for firms with 100 to 299 employees, and 84.3 percent for firms with 30 to 99 employees. Over the past two decades, however, many firms with a uniform retirement age system have been extending the

retirement age from fifty-five years or less to sixty years, regardless of
sex or occupational classification. While only 32.3 percent of firms had
a uniform retirement age of sixty years in 1976, this percentage has
increased to 80 percent today and reaches as high as 90 percent if firms
that plan to extend retirement age to sixty years in the near future are
included. The Japanese Ministry of Labor currently encourages all firms
and organizations to adopt a retirement age policy of sixty years and
will soon make this an enforceable regulation. The Council on Aging
Society of the Ministry further recommends that those workers over the
age of sixty years who desire to continue working should be able to do
so. This new consideration is expected to be incorporated into the formal
regulation by the early part of the twenty-first century.[9]

PROBLEMS CONCERNING ELDERLY EMPLOYMENT

There are two problems concerning employment of the elderly in Japan. First, there are substantially more elderly workers seeking employment than firms who wish to hire them. In 1989 the overall labor force
ratio in Japan was 1.39, indicating substantially more demand for workers than supply. But when broken down by age, these ratios drop to 0.44
for workers between fifty-five and fifty-nine years of age and to as low
as 0.21 for those between sixty and sixty-four years of age.[10] These
numbers clearly confirm that the elderly workforce is not in demand in
the Japanese labor market today.

Nevertheless, labor force participation rates among the elderly in Japan
are much higher than those of their Western counterparts. In 1992, 409
million people sixty-five years and older (25.4 percent) were in the labor
force. In the case of elderly men, nearly four in ten (38.2 percent) were
working, compared to 16.1 percent in the United States, 11.4 percent in
Canada, 8.6 percent in the United Kingdom, 8.0 percent in Italy, 5.2
percent in Germany, and 2.8 percent in France.[11]

A second problem is that the total unemployment rate of the elderly
workforce is significantly higher than the overall rate. In 1992, for example, the total unemployment rate across all age groups was 2.2 percent, while for workers between the ages of sixty and sixty-four years it
was 4.7 percent. Given the strong orientation among Japanese firms to
hire younger workers, it is extremely difficult for the elderly to become
reemployed once they retire from a job.[12]

There are several reasons why Japanese firms are reluctant to hire elderly workers. First, employers are greatly concerned about the ability of elderly workers to perform the required tasks. Employers find that elderly workers often lack not only physical strength but also flexibility in thinking. Compared with younger workers, they have less curiosity, spirit, and innovation, the qualities that Japanese employers look for at the time of recruitment. Second, workers over the age of sixty tend to require more individual attention than younger workers. Since most Japanese firms are accustomed to following one uniform labor management program that can be applied to all the employees, they are ill-equipped to provide individual care to an older workforce. Third, limited job opportunities, the high cost of salaries, and unsuitable work conditions tend to hinder the recruitment of elderly workers. These factors have become even more debilitating with the prolonged economic recession in Japan beginning in the summer of 1991.

However, many elderly workers believe that they could make a productive contribution to the workforce if employers were willing to improve work conditions by offering alternative work plans. Such plans might include shorter work hours, flex-time, and work-sharing programs for elderly workers. As the aging of Japan continues, it is clear that industry and society will benefit by redefining the definition of what makes a worker productive and, in so doing, to cultivate a more positive attitude toward an elderly workforce.

THE SILVER MARKET[13]

One positive, new way of viewing the Japanese elderly is as vital consumers in a large and growing silver market. In Japan, people over fifty-five years of age are generally referred to as "silver citizens." Industry has adopted this term in its newfound effort to make products that are particularly attractive to the silver market. No longer considered merely a group of people with too much time on their hands, silver citizens have emerged as an important and growing sector of the nation's consumers possessing highly stable purchasing power.

In order to better meet the needs of this important group of post-retirement citizens, industries are gearing up to provide a greater range of goods and services in such areas as health foods and sports to improve physical fitness, fashions suitable for advanced age and social standing, specially designed housing to keep up with the rising number of elderly singles and couples, cultural appreciation, education and leisure activi-

Figure 9–1
Changes in the Growth of the Silver Market by Industry: 1980–2000

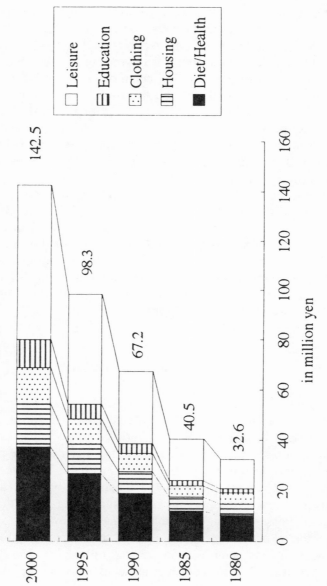

in million yen

Source: Kumagai, 1985b, 46.

ties, and diversification of investment portfolios designed to ensure a stable income.

The silver market is projected to more than quadruple its size from 1980 to the year 2000 (see Figure 9–1). While areas of consumption related to basic necessities, such as diet, housing, and clothes, are expected to contract, other areas, such as education and leisure, are projected to expand dramatically over the next two decades. These trends will be further affected by the growing number of baby boomers who will enter the silver market by the year 2000. These new silver consumers will have lifestyles vastly different from those of today's silver citizens who grew up according to Japan's traditional culture and ideology. A great majority of the soon-to-be-aged will be salaried men with at least a high school education who have been engaged in the working force in either secondary or tertiary industries. Clearly, new marketing strategies will be required to meet the needs of this changing elderly population.

Market analyses reveal that the products with greatest potential are those related to basic life needs such as health and medical care, those affecting economic security, and those tied to spiritual fulfillment and enjoyment of life. A productive silver market strategy, therefore, might be to ensure that the elderly can enjoy balanced lives that incorporate a variety of products in the context of their total life planning.

The concept of total life planning is currently attracting great attention in the United States. It involves making decisions about career and retirement throughout one's entire life course and thus differs markedly from the past practice of planning one's postretirement life just shortly before retirement age. The principal silver market strategy of the future will aim at increasing awareness of the need for total life planning through this stage-by-stage method. In light of the extremely rapid aging of Japanese society, this type of long-range planning will prove essential for the well-being of Japan's elderly population.

NOTES

1. Institute of Population Problems, 1993a, 189, table 26.
2. Ibid.
3. Ibid., 103–104, tables 8–3 and 8–4; Women's Bureau of the Ministry of Labor, 1993b, supplementary table 2.
4. Office of Aging, Prime Minister's Office, 1991, 11–13, tables 8–11.
5. Prime Minister's Office, 1990b.

6. Management and Coordination Agency, Office of Aging, 1991, 13, table 11.

7. Prime Minister's Office, 1993d, 17–18, table 7.

8. Hayashi, 1994.

9. Ministry of Labor, Council on Aging, 1993b.

10. Statistical Bureau of the Prime Minister's Office, 1993, 5, table 4.

11. Office of Aging, Prime Minister's Office, 1991.

12. Women's Bureau of the Ministry of Labor, 1993b, supplementary table 8; Institute of Population Problems, 1993a.

13. This section is a summary of "Japan's 'silver market' and aging society." See Kumagai, 1985. For more detail, please refer to the original article.

CHAPTER 10

The Impact of Aging on Family Relations

Societal aging has important implications not only for the elderly themselves but for their families. This is especially true in Japan, where the traditional ideals of family life continue to play a critical role in Japanese society. Adult children and their families, especially the sons' families, are expected to extend support to their elderly parents by providing them a place to live.

LIVING ARRANGEMENTS FOR THE ELDERLY

In modern Japan the coresidence rate for the elderly, or the proportion of the elderly over sixty-five years of age who reside with their children and/or relatives, has always been high compared to that of Western societies.[1] Today slightly less than six out of every ten elderly persons adopt coresidence living arrangements (see Figure 10–1). Although still quite high, the percentage is significantly lower than thirty years ago when 86.8 percent of Japan's elderly coresided with their families.[2] Living arrangements for the Japanese elderly vary according to marital status, sex, age and the community in which one resides.[3] Several trends may be identified. First, the rate of coresidency increases as the elderly

Figure 10–1
Changes in Living Arrangements of the Elderly Sixty-Five and Over: 1960–1990

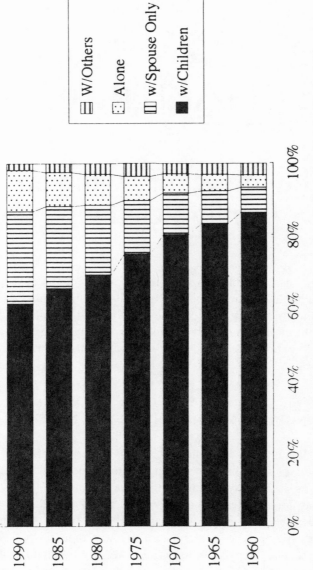

Sources: Statistical Bureau of the Management and Coordination Agency, *Kokuseichosa Hokoku* (National Census Reports), reported in the Institute of Population Problems, Ministry of Health and Welfare, 1990, 80, table 8–17 for 1960, 1965, 1970, 1975, 1980, and 1985 statistics; Statistical Bureau of the Ministry of Health and Welfare, 1993a, 14–15, tables 8 and 9, for 1992.

get older, ranging from 49.5 percent for those between sixty-five and sixty-nine years of age to 72.6 percent for those eighty years and older.[4] Second, elderly living in urban areas are less likely to live with their children's family and more likely to live with a spouse or alone. Third, the coresidence rate of elderly women has always been higher than that of men, and the gap becomes more apparent as elderly women grow older. This is because women tend to live longer than men and have spouses who are older than they are. In 1991, for example, 78.2 percent of elderly women aged eighty years or more lived in coresidency, compared to 63.0 percent of elderly men of a similar age.[5] Furthermore, women are less likely than men to live with their spouse only and more likely to live with children or alone.

Although the proportion of the elderly living alone in Japan has been increasing (from 1.1 percent in 1960 to 4.4 percent in 1992),[6] the number is still quite small, especially among those who suffer from ill health. The rate of increase for elderly couples living alone (7.0 percent in 1960 to 22.8 percent in 1992) has been more significant than that of noninstitutionalized elderly living alone (3.8 percent in 1960 to 15.7 percent in 1992).[7]

When asked about their desired lifestyles in old age, more than half (54.3 percent) of the Japanese men and women respondents between the ages of thirty and fifty-nine preferred to live independently from their children's families. Of them, 41.4 percent wished to maintain close family relationships, while the remaining preferred to keep their lives quite independent of relatives.[8] As expected, the desire for coresidency living arrangements was much higher for people in rural towns and villages (52.2 percent), nearly twice as many as those in urban areas such as Tokyo (28.7 percent). These results suggest that rural-urban variations in terms of attitudes toward old age persist in the minds of Japanese today.[9]

REASONS FOR THE HIGH CORESIDENCE RATE

The high coresidency rate of the elderly in Japan is regarded by many as a unique characteristic of Japanese society. Whether it is due to traditional sociocultural aspects of the Japanese family system or simply inadequate social support policies for the elderly is unclear.

Tradition of Family Support for the Elderly

As mentioned previously, nearly half of the Japanese people prefer multigenerational family life over nuclear family life (25 percent) or families consisting of spouses only (12 percent). While this preference for multigenerational living arrangements may reflect the Japanese people's traditional attitudes toward the family, it may also be true that there are few workable alternatives. While the majority (75.3 percent) of Japanese people today still believe that it is their duty to support their frail elderly parents, slightly more than half of those between the ages of thirty and sixty-nine years, and an increasing number of the younger generation (59.5 percent of men and 56.0 percent of women in the thirty to thirty-four age bracket versus 48.1 percent of men and 54.0 percent of women in the fifty-five to fifty-nine age bracket), would prefer to live apart from their elderly parents. This trend suggests that Japanese young people have started to appreciate an independent lifestyle in old age, attitudes that may help to foster more positive interaction between younger and older generations.

Perhaps because the majority (84 percent) of Japan's elderly reside with the son's family, attitudes toward coresidency differ between men and women: Only 42.8 percent of women versus 47.6 percent of men between fifty-five and fifty-nine years of age consider coresidency the optimal living arrangement, whereas 40.1 percent of women versus 39.7 percent of men between thirty and thirty-four years of age prefer not to do so.[10] As they age, however, both men and women are more inclined to favor coresidency living arrangements. In fact, more than half of Japanese men and women in their sixties consider coresidency to be an agreeable lifestyle in their old age.

Of those who do not favor coresidency living arrangements, the majority (63.0 percent) would still prefer to live in the same neighborhood as their children's family, whereas only a quarter would prefer to remain completely independent. Slightly more women (43.4 percent) prefer to remain close to their children's families than men do (38.8 percent).[11]

Preferred Living Arrangements for Japanese

In Western societies, the desired rate of coresidency in old age is considerably lower than in Japan.[12] More than half (53.6 percent) of

Japanese adults and nearly two thirds (61.4 percent) of Koreans desire to live with their children's families when they become old. Only a small proportion of adults in Western societies feel the same way (United States: 3.4 percent; United Kingdom: 3.4 percent; and Germany: 15.4 percent). Although Westerners prefer independent living arrangements, they still want to maintain strong family ties through visits and frequent communication (72.7 percent in the United States, 73.2 percent in the United Kingdom, and 55.3 percent in Germany versus 37.8 percent in Japan and 33.9 percent in Korea).

These findings suggest that Eastern peoples adhere to the traditional ideology of filial piety much more than their Western counterparts. Nevertheless, the impact of modern lifestyles on those in Eastern societies is evident in the declining rates of desire for coresidency arrangements. In Japan, nearly six out of ten (59.4 percent) Japanese adults preferred such arrangements in 1981, but in 1990 only slightly half did so. (In Korea these proportions were 83.3 percent in 1981 versus 61.4 percent in 1990.)[13] In fact, it may be the Japanese elderly themselves who are increasingly reluctant to spend their later years living with the families of their children.

Lack of Other Alternatives

In addition to traditional Japanese family values, there may be several other explanations for the remarkably high coresidency rate of the Japanese elderly. First, financial problems of the elderly may force them to depend on their children's families. Second, the lack of housing, especially in urban areas, may leave the elderly with little choice but to reside with their children's families. Third, coresidency living arrangements can benefit the children's family. Especially in dual-career families where both husband and wife work outside the home, the elderly can act as a housesitter or babysitter and also help with household chores.

It is certainly conceivable that many of the Japanese elderly who adopt coresidency living arrangements today do so not out of choice but out of necessity. Although living in multigenerational households may provide the elderly with a supportive family environment in their time of need, it is no doubt stressful to have to depend on one's family because constrained economic resources prevent independent living.

INTERGENERATIONAL CONFLICTS

During the prewar period when life expectancy was much shorter, successive generations of families coresided for much briefer periods of time. Consequently, generational conflicts among household members were minimal. Today the stress of prolonged multigenerational living arrangements has resulted in intense intergenerational conflicts that reveal the ongoing struggle between traditional attitudes and modern lifestyles in Japan today, particularly since adjustment to new lifestyles is extremely difficult for the older generation. In addition, the strong intergenerational ties that existed between mother and son in times past can be a continuing source of friction for young wives who must cope with their mothers-in-law on a daily live-in basis.

Although there is no ideal solution for the intergenerational problems that can accompany coresidency living arrangements, a number of alternative living arrangements might alleviate these conflicts. First, quasi-coresidence living arrangements, such as the maintenance of separate living quarters under one roof or living in neighboring towns so that regular visitations are possible, might be preferable to complete coresidency. Under these circumstances, both the elderly and their children's families could maintain their privacy while still sharing close contact in everyday life.

Elderly parents might also consider residing with the families of their daughters instead of those of their sons. Conflicts between blood relatives, such as elderly mothers and their married daughters, might prove more manageable than those between in-laws.

A third alternative would be for the children's families to take turns supporting their elderly parents. Although the elderly parents would not have a permanent place of residency, shorter-term stays in each of their children's homes might result in more positive intergenerational relationships.

The American case is instructive in this regard. Despite the lower rates of coresidency in the United States, many younger generation Americans are willing to extend support to their elderly parents and prefer to maintain close contacts with them. In fact, empirical studies prove the existence of strong and cohesive intergenerational relationships among American families despite their low rates of coresidency. When facing financial hardship, two thirds of the American elderly seek assistance from their children and other relatives (63.2 percent) and one quarter from their spouses (24.4 percent). In Japan, on the other hand, more than half of the elderly (53.7 percent) rely on their spouses for financial support, and the remaining (42.9 percent) turn to their coresiding children.[14]

Nevertheless, Japanese people have yet to establish close and mutually rewarding marital relationships. Although an extremely high proportion (86.1 percent) of Japanese today believe that elderly couples can have satisfactory lives together and would try to spend more time in joint activities (77.2 percent), their concerns are also evident. One third of Japanese married couples (30.6 percent) feel that they would have no hobbies in common; 12.7 percent indicate that they would be too busy to find the time to enjoy activities with their spouses; and 10.5 percent would actually be uneasy in the presence of their marriage partners.[15] Clearly, Japanese couples must learn how to lead active lives with their marriage partners that will sustain them through old age.

POLICIES FOR ENHANCING INTERGENERATIONAL COOPERATION

While encouraging the elderly to enjoy more independent lifestyles as long as they are able to do so may result in stronger intergenerational cooperation, increased public support for coresidency arrangements should also be considered. Since the most serious problems of coresidency stem from the financial burdens placed on the custodial family, government programs such as Aid for Families with Dependent Elderly (AFDE), similar to the Aid for Families with Dependent Children (AFDC) in the United States, might alleviate much of the stress inherent in coresidency.

Despite the extremely rapid aging of the Japanese population, no integrated social policies have yet been proposed. In 1990, the government set forth a ''10-Year Strategy to Promote Health Care and Welfare for the Elderly,'' the so-called Golden Plan. Under this plan, the government aims to develop an infrastructure for public services in health care and welfare for the elderly that includes various types of welfare facilities to meet the needs of the elderly and their families.[16]

Nevertheless, it has been the family, and more particularly the women, who support and care for the elderly in Japan, not the state. Three-generation living arrangements have been successful only because Japanese women have been willing to sacrifice their careers and social status in order to assume the traditional responsibility of caring for the elderly.

But as more and more middle-aged women decide to reenter or remain in the labor force, they will have to relinquish their role as full-time care provider for elderly parents. Therefore, the state and society must assume greater responsibility for the welfare of the Japanese elderly.

A recent study revealed that the number of Japanese elderly who participate in some form of volunteer activity remains fractional, although percentages have increased from 2.9 in 1988 to 4.2 in 1993.[17] In fact, some communities have developed social participation programs for the elderly, including a so-called volunteer hour-saving program (or volunteer coupon program) that allows able elderly persons to accumulate hours by participating in volunteer activities. When in need of assistance, this volunteer can receive services commensurate with his or her contribution. Since such programs have not yet been well publicized, only four out of ten Japanese elderly (41.6 percent) are actually aware of them, but two thirds (65.4 percent) feel that such programs should be developed further.[18] Clearly, these nonfamilial support programs for the care of the elderly should be implemented on a much wider basis.

Family relations in Japan's aging society will undoubtedly undergo substantial change and modification in the years to come. Although a variety of social support structures for the elderly must be considered, traditional value systems that place this responsibility on the family are certain to persist well into the future.

NOTES

1. In the United States in 1979, only 9.8 percent of elderly men and 21.9 percent of elderly women lived with someone other than their spouses, most commonly with children (Bureau of the Census, 1980, 34). Furthermore, in 1987, over 30 percent of the noninstitutionalized American elderly sixty-five years and older live alone, and only about 5 percent of the American elderly reside in nursing homes (Soldo and Agree, 1988, 30).

2. Changes over time in the proportion of the elderly who adopt coresidence housing arrangements were as follows: 1960: 86.8 percent; 1965: 83.8 percent; 1970: 79.6 percent; 1975: 74.4 percent; 1980: 69.8 percent; 1985: 65.5 percent; 1989: 60.0 percent; 1992: 57.1 percent. See Shishido, 1987; Institute of Population Problems, 1990, 80, table 8–17; Statistical Bureau of the Ministry of Health and Welfare, 1993a, 14–15, tables 8 and 9.

3. Hiroshima, 1987; Kumagai, 1987a.

4. Institute of Population Problems, 1993a, 96, table 7–19; Statistical Bureau of the Ministry of Health and Welfare, 1993a, 15, tables 9, 16, 20.

5. Statistical Bureau of the Ministry of Health and Welfare, 1992, 7, table 8.

6. Statistical Bureau of the Ministry of Health and Welfare, 1993a, 11, table 5.

7. Institute of Population Problems, 1993a, 96, table 7–19; Statistical Bureau of the Ministry of Health and Welfare, 1993a, 14, table 8.

8. Prime Minister's Office, 1994a, 28–29, table 11. The interview survey was conducted in September 1993, and a total of 2,277 (men: 1,000; women: 1,277) between thirty and fifty-nine years of age responded with a response rate of 75.9 percent.

9. Ibid., 102, table 12.

10. Ibid.

11. Ibid.

12. Office of Aging, Prime Minister's Office, 1991, 8, table 5.

13. Office of Aging, Prime Minister's Office, 1991.

14. Management and Coordination Agency, 1991, 9–10, table 10.

15. Prime Minister's Office, 1994a, 25–27, table 10, figure 10.

16. K. Hayashi, 1994, 6–7.

17. Office of Aging, Prime Minister's Office, 1993, 11. Interviews with men and women sixty years and older were conducted in February 1993 throughout Japan, tapping the social participation/activities of Japanese elderly. The first such study was conducted in 1988.

18. Ibid., 21–22, tables I–32 and I–34.

Conclusion: From Modernization to Internationalization

Modern-day Japan has proven to be a complex nation struggling to combine traditional attitudes and mores with the political and social demands of an advanced industrialized economy. As discussed above, this struggle to balance the past with the present has had a significant impact on the structure of human relations in Japan, particularly in the areas of family dynamics and lifestyles, education and socialization of youth, the role of women, and support for the elderly. In all cases, we find a dual structure where traditional values and modern practices coexist.

As an emerging world leader, the struggle to define and shape the structure of human relations in Japan today is becoming even more complex, involving not only elements of the past and present within Japan but a new set of forces imposed by the process of Japan's internationalization. As in the past phases of its modernization, Japan must once again learn to adapt its practices to the accepted norms of the international arena while at the same time retaining those customs and values from which it will continue to benefit. The effort of Japanese families abroad to accommodate their lifestyles and values to those of the communities in which they reside provides just one example of this ongoing struggle.

THE ISSUE OF CULTURE IN
INTERNATIONALIZATION

Internationalization emerged as a primary goal of the Japanese in the 1980s. For the most part, however, internationalization has meant simply learning foreign languages, traveling overseas, or studying abroad in order to gain knowledge of advanced technologies and has only just begun to include opening Japanese culture to outside influences by welcoming foreigners to study, work, or live in Japan. In this sense, Japan has remained an exclusionist country where foreigners continue to be referred to as *gaijin*, or outsiders. Much as it has in the past, Japan has chosen a selective course of internationalization: learning what it can from the outside while retaining its own cultural uniqueness on the inside.

Unfortunately, Japan's inwardly closed society has resulted in a number of cross-cultural communication gaps between Japanese and other peoples. Indeed, a growing number of scholars and others who are concerned about international relations have begun to point to the significance of cultural factors in maintaining positive relations among nations. Iriye, for example, has argued that culture plays a far more important role today than it did in the past, when issues of national defense, diplomacy, and trade tended to dominate the international agenda.[1] Culture itself has become a tool with which nations can communicate beyond the boundaries of parochial nationalism.[2]

Recognizing that intercultural understanding is essential to resolving such issues as the trade imbalance and the north-south problem, governments of leading nations have already begun to increase their efforts to promote international cultural exchanges. Although individual nations will certainly retain their own culture-specific orientations, they must learn to come together as equal partners on a fair and equitable international playing field.

TOWARD THE SUCCESSFUL
INTERNATIONALIZATION OF JAPAN

Only through cross-cultural experiences will the Japanese people be able to recognize the differences that exist between modern Western societies and Japan and to learn from them. In this process, the best of Japanese tradition can be maintained while significant progress can be made in a number of areas previously stalled in the name of tradition, most notably, balanced and spiritually fulfilling lifestyles, creative and innovative education for the young, equality for women at work and at home, and support structures for the elderly.

While these are but a few of the facets of contemporary Japanese society presented in an effort to unmask the Japan that we know today, the contrasts and parallels between tradition and modernity are quite telling. As Japan proceeds in its transformation from a world economic power to becoming a truly global partner, the need of the Japanese people to identify themselves with others in the world will become even more urgent. At the same time, the unique sociocultural characteristics of what it means to be "Japanese" will come into play. For the harmonious coexistence of tradition and modernity is not only the essence of Japanese society but the impetus for Japan's impending internationalization.

And by opening Japanese culture and traditions to outsiders, perhaps other nations will come to understand how to achieve a better balance between the elements of tradition and modernity within their own societies. Strong family values, the importance of education, and respect for the elderly need not exist separate and apart from economic growth. Thus, Japan's quest for internationalization may become a process not only of learning from its equally advanced neighbors but of sharing with them all that it has come to know.

NOTES

1. Iriye, 1989, 62–63.
2. Kato, et al., 1989, 66.

References

Abbey, Antonia, and Frank M. Andrews. 1985. ''Modeling the psychological determinants of life quality.'' *Social Indicators Research* 16: 1–34.

Abbey, Antonia, C. Dunkel–Schetter, and P. Brickman. 1983. ''Handling the stress of looking for a job in law school; the relationship between intrinsic motivation, internal attributions, relations with others, and happiness.'' *Basic and Applied Social Psychology* 4: 263–278.

Agency for Cultural Affairs. 1988. *Yearbook on Religion.* Tokyo: Government Printing Office.

Agnew, Robert, and Sandra Huguley. 1989. ''Adolescent violence toward parents.'' *Journal of Marriage and the Family* 51 (August): 699–711.

Aida, Yuji. 1972. *Nihonjin no Ishiki Kozo* (The Structure of the Japanese Consciousness). Tokyo: Kodansha.

Allardt, E. 1976. ''Dimensions of welfare in a comparative Scandinavian study.'' *Acta Sociologica* 19:111–120.

Allen, G.C. 1987. *Modern Japan and Its Problems.* Chicago: Athlone Press.

Alwin, Duane F., Philip E. Converse, and Steven S. Martin. 1986. ''Living arrangements and social integration.'' Chap. 11, 271–299, in *Research on the Quality of Life*, ed. Frank M. Andrews. Ann Arbor: Survey Research Center—Institute for Social Research, University of Michigan.

Amaya, Naohiro. 1990. ''The ugly Japanese?'' *Intersect* (August): 36–38.

Andrews, Frank M., and S. B. Withey. 1976. *Social Indicators of Well–Being: Americans' Perceptions of Life Quality.* New York: Plenum.

Aoki, Tamotsu. 1990. *Nihon Bunkaron no Henyo* (Changes in the Theories of Japanese Culture). Tokyo: Chuo Koron–sha.

Arisawa, Hiromi. 1957. "Nihon keizai no kindaika to koyo" (Modernization of Japanese economy and employment practices). *Seisansei Kojo Series* (Improving Productivity), 70. (Special lecture for the second anniversary of the establishment of the Japan Productivity Promotion Center.)

Ariyoshi, Sawako. 1984. *The Twilight Years.* Translated by M. Tahara. New York: Kodansha International.

Asahi Shimbun. 1993. *Japan Almanac, 1994.* Tokyo: Asahi Shimbun.

Asahi Shimbun. 1994. *Japan Almanac, 1995.* Tokyo: Asahi Shimbun.

Association of Colleges and Universities in the Greater Tokyo Metropolitan Area. 1994. "Shutoken geshuku shidaisei keihi chosa" (Household expenditures of college students living alone in the Tokyo area in 1993). April.

Atal, Yogesh. 1989. "Outsiders as insiders: The phenomenon of sandwich culture—prefatorial to a possible theory." Mimeographed.

Bachman, Jerald G., Lloyd D. Johnston, and Patrick M. O'Malley. 1986. "Recent findings from monitoring the future: A continuing study of the life-styles and values of youth." Chap. 8, 215–233 in *Research on the Quality of Life,* ed. Frank M. Andrews. Ann Arbor: Survey Research Center—Institute for Social Research, University of Michigan.

Barber, William J. 1961. *The Economy of British Central Africa.* Stanford: Stanford University Press.

Barnlund, Dean C., ed., *Interpersonal Communication: Survey and Studies.* Boston: Houghton Mifflin.

Barnlund, Dean C. 1989. *Communicative Styles of Japanese and Americans: Images and Realities.* Wadsworth, CA: Wadsworth Publishing.

Battered Wives' Study Group. 1993. "Tsuma gyakutai chosa hokoku" (Study report on battered wives), reported in the *Japan Economic Journal,* August 3 morning edition.

Beauchamp, Edward R., ed., 1978. *Learning to Be Japanese: Selected Readings on Japanese Society and Education.* New York: Linnet Books.

Billings, A. G., and R. H. Moos. 1981. "The role of coping responses and social resources in attenuating the stress of life events." *Journal of Behavioral Medicine* 2: 139–157.

Blau, Z. S. 1981. *Aging in a Changing Society.* 2nd ed. New York: Franklin Watts.

Boeke, Julius H. 1930. *Dualistische Economie.* Leiden: S. C. van Doesburgh.

Boeke, Julius H. 1942. *The Structure of Netherlands Indian Economy.* New York: AMS Press.

Boeke, Julius H. 1953. *Economics and Economic Policy of Dual Societies: As Exemplified by Indonesia.* New York: Institute of Pacific Relations, International Secretariat.

Bonacich, Edna. 1973. "A theory of middleman minorities." *American Sociological Review* 38, (5): 583–589.

Bradburn, N. M. 1969. *The Structure of Psychological Well–Being.* Chicago: Aldine.

Breitenbach, Diether. 1970. "The evaluation of study abroad." Pp.70–98 in *Students as Links between Cultures: A Cross Cultural Survey Based on UNESCO Studies,* ed. Ingrid Eide. Oslo: Scandinavian University Books.

Bryant, Fred B., and Joseph Veroff. 1984. "Dimensions of subjective mental health in American men and women." *Journal of Health and Social Behavior* 25: 116–135.

Bureau of Health and Social Welfare for the Elderly, Ministry of Health and Welfare. 1994. "Zenkoku 100–sai ijo chosa" (National survey of the elderly 100 and over). November.

Bureau of the Census, U.S. Department of Commerce,Economics and Statistics Administration. 1980. *Statistical Abstract of the United States: 1980.* 100th ed. Washington, D.C.: U.S. Government Printing Office.

Bureau of Women, Ministry of Labor. 1994. "Fujin shonen mondai shingikai fujinbukai chukanhokoku ni tsuite" (Interim report of the Committee on Women's Issues). January.

Burgess, Eugene W. 1958. "The family in changing society." *American Journal of Sociology 53 (6): 417–422.*

Burks, Ardath W. 1981. *Japan: Profile of a Postindustrial Power.* Boulder, CO: Westview Press.

Business Week. 1989. "Rethinking Japan." August 7.

Campbell, Angus. 1980. *The Sense of Well–Being in America: Recent Patterns and Trends.* New York: McGraw–Hill.

Campbell, Angus, P. E. Converse, and W. L. Rodgers. 1976. *The Quality of American Life: Perceptions, Evaluations, and Satisfactions.* New York: Russell Sage Foundation.

Campbell, R. 1967. "Violence in adolescence." *Journal of Analytic Psychology* 12: 161–173.

Caplan, R. D. 1979. "Social support, person–environment fit, and coping." Pp. 89–137 in *Mental Health and the Economy,* ed. L. A. Ferman and J. P. Gordus. Kalamazoo, MI: Upjohn Institute.

Center for Disease Control and Prevention, National Center for Health Statistics. 1994. *Monthly Vital Statistics Report.*

Charles, Andrew V. 1986. "Physically abused parents." *Journal of Family Violence* 4: 343–355.

Chikushi, Tetsuya. 1986. "Young people as a new human race." *Japan Quarterly* 33, (3): 291–294.

Christopher, Robert C. 1983. *The Japanese Mind.* New York: Fawcett Columbine–Ballantine Books/Random House.

Clayton, R. R. 1979. *The Family, Marriage and Social Change.* 2nd ed. Lexington, MA: D. C. Heath.

Collcutt, Martin, Marius Jansen, and Isao Kumakura. 1988. *Cultural Atlas of Japan*. New York: Facts on File Publications.

The Community. 1989. No. 85 Special Issue on "Internationalization and the Japanese language." Tokyo: Chiiki Shakai Kenkyujo (Institute of Community Relations).

Condon, James. 1987. *With Respect to the Japanese: A Guide for Americans*. Washington, D.C.: Sietar International Publications.

Cornell, Claire P., and Richard J. Gelles. 1982. "Adolescent to parent violence." *Urban and Social Change Review* 15: 8–14.

Coughlin, R. J. 1960. *Double Identity: The Chinese in Modern Thailand*. Hong Kong: Hong Kong University Press.

Courdy, Jean-Claude. 1984. *The Japanese: Everyday Life in the Empire of the Rising Sun*. Translated from the French edition by Raymond Rosenthal, New York: Harper & Row, Publishers. Original work published in 1979.

Craft, Lucille. 1991. "Class struggle." *PHP*. (March): 8–11.

Cunningham, Hisako. 1988. *Kaigaishijyokyoiku Jijyo* (Japanese Children's Education Abroad). Tokyo: Shincho–sha.

Current Anthropology. 1987. *An Anthropological Profile of Japan*, vol.28 (4).

Dahrendorf, Ralph. 1959. *Class and Class Conflict in Industrial Society*. Stanford: Stanford University Press.

Dai–Hyaku Life Insurance Co. 1990. "Shufu no rogo ni kansuru ishiki" (Attitudes of housewives toward old age).

Daini Den Den, K. K. 1993. "DDI, Talk" in *0077*, vol.42.

Doi, Takeo. 1962. "Amae: A key concept for understanding Japanese personality." Pp. 132–139 in *Japanese Culture: Its Development and Characteristics*, ed. R. J. Smith and R. K. Beardsley. New York: Aldine.

Doi, Takeo. 1971. *The Anatomy of Dependence*. Tokyo: Kodansha International, Ltd.

Doi, Takeo. 1985. *Omote to Ura* (The Front and the Back). Tokyo: Kobu-ndo.

Domoto, Akiko. 1987. "Student returnees, student misfits." *Japan Quarterly* 34 (1): 34–38.

Dore, Ronald P. 1973. *British Factory, Japanese Factory*. Berkeley: University of California Press.

Economic Planning Agency. 1986. "Choju shakai he muketeno seikatsu sentaku" (Alternative lifestyles in the era of aging society).

Economic Planning Agency. 1989. *White Paper on the National Life*. November 30.

Economic Planning Agency. 1990. *White Paper on the Economy*.

Economic Planning Agency. 1992. *White Paper on the National Life* (Impact of Low Fertility Society).

Economic Planning Agency. 1993. *White Paper on the National Life* (Human Interactions).

Economic Planning Agency. 1994a. "Hatarakisugi to kenko shogai" (Health–related problems caused by working too hard). January.

Economic Planning Agency. 1994b. "Heisei 5–nendo kokumin seikatsu senkodo chosa" (Public opinion survey on the preference and choice of the Japanese people's life). February.

The Economist. 1990. "Japan's schools: Why can't little Taro think?" (April 21): 19–22.

Enomoto, M. 1973. "Kazoku hendo to sono ijo: Kateinai ranboo shonen o megutte" (Family change and its abnormality: filial violence). Pp.115–132 in *Kazokuhendo no Shakaigaku* (Sociology of Family Change), ed. Kazuo Aoi and Kokichi Masuda, Tokyo: Baifukan.

Esaka, Akira, and Kimindo Kusaka. 1990. "Farewell to the corporate warrior." *Japan Echo* 17, (Special Issue): 37–41.

Etzioni, Amitai, and Eva Etzioni–Halevy, eds. 1973. *Social Change: Sources, Patterns, and Consequences.* 2nd ed. New York: Basic Books.

Fallows, James. 1989a. "Containing Japan." *The Atlantic Monthly.* May.

Fallows, James. 1989b. *More Like Us: Making America Great Again.* Boston: Houghton Mifflin.

Farkas, Jennifer B., and Morio Kono. 1987. *America no Nihonjin Seito Tachi* (Japanese Children in America). Tokyo: Tokyo Shoseki.

Federation of Employees Unions of the Metropolitan Tokyo Area Private Colleges and Universities 1994. "1993-nendo shiritsu daigaku shin'nyusei no kakeihi futan chosa" (Household expenditures for college freshmen enrolled in private institutions in 1993). April.

French, J. R. P., Jr., W. Rodgers, and S. Cobb. 1974. "Adjustment as person-environment fit." Pp. 316–333 in *Coping and Adaptation*, ed. G. V. Coelho, D. A. Hamburg, and J. E. Adams. New York: Basic Books.

Fuji Economic Research Institute. 1982. "Marketing strategy in a maturing society."

Fujioka, Wakao. 1989. "Learning to live the good life." *Japan Echo* 16 (2): 30–34.

Fukazawa, Shichiro. 1956. *Narayama-Bushi-Ko.* Tokyo: Kodanshei.

Fukutake, Tadashi. 1980. *Rural Society in Japan.* Tokyo: University of Tokyo Press.

Fukutake, Tadashi. 1981. *Japanese Society Today.* 2nd ed. Tokyo: University of Tokyo Press.

Furnivall, John S. 1939. *Netherlands India: A Study of Plural Economy.* Cambridge: Cambridge University Press.

Furnivall, John S. 1948. *Colonial Policy and Practice: A Comparative Study of Burma and the Netherlands.* Cambridge: Cambridge University Press.

Gamo, Masao. 1960. *Nihonjin no Seikatsu Kozo Josetsu* (Life Structure of the Japanese People). Tokyo: Seishin-shobo.

Gilmartin, K. J., R. S. Rossi, L. S. Lutomski, and D. F. B. Reed. 1979. *Social Indicators: An Annotated Bibliography of Current Literature.* Ann Arbor: Survey Research Center, Institute for Social Research, University of Michigan.

Glick, Paul C. 1977. "Updating the life cycle of the family." *Journal of Marriage and the Family* 39 (February): 5–13.

Goode, William J. 1963. *World Revolution and Family Patterns.* New York: Free Press.

Gurin, G., Joseph Veroff, and S. Feld. 1960. *Americans View Their Mental Health.* New York: Basic Books.

Hagiwara, Shigeru. 1990. "Can we really talk in Japanese?" *Japan Quarterly* 37 (2): 158–163.

Hall, Edward T., and Mildred Reed Hall. 1987. *Hidden Differences: Doing Business with the Japanese.* New York: Anchor Press/Doubleday.

Hamaguchi, Eshun. 1980. "Nihonjin no rentaiteki jiritsusei—kanjin shugi to kojin shugi" (Joint autonomy of the Japanese—corporatism vs. individualism). Pp.127–140 in *Shudanshugi* (Groupism), ed. Eshun Hamaguchi. Tokyo: Shibundo.

Harbin, Henry T., and Dennis J. Madden. 1979. "Battered parents: A new syndrome." *American Journal of Psychiatry* 136: 1288–1291.

Hasegawa, Kazuo. 1987. "Chiho towa nanika?" (What is senile dementia?) Chap. 6, 72–83 in *Kaso to Kamitsu ni Ikiru Sansedai no Nihonjin* (Three Generations of the Japanese in the Underpopulated and Overpopulated Regions: For the Construction of an Integrated Social System), ed. Fumie Kumagai. Tokyo: Toyota Foundation.

Hayashi, Kenji. 1994. "The role of women in the aging society of Japan—present and future issues." Paper presented at the Population Aging Workshop of UNFPA, JOICFP, University of Singapore, March 14–17.

Hayashi, Shuji. 1988. *Culture and Management in Japan.* Tokyo: University of Tokyo Press.

Headey, B. 1981. "The quality of life in Australia." *Social Indicators Research* 9: 155–181.

Hendry, Joy. 1987. *Understanding Japanese Society.* London: Croom Helm.

Herzog, A. Regula, and Willard L. Rodgers. 1986. "Satisfaction among older adults." Chap. 9, 235–251, in *Research on the Quality of Life*, ed. Frank M. Andrews. Ann Arbor: Survey Research Center—Institute for Social Research, University of Michigan.

Higgins, Benjamin J. 1956. "The 'dualistic theory' of underdeveloped areas." *Economic Development and Cultural Change* 4 (Jan.): 99–115.

Hiroshima, Kiyoshi. 1987. "Recent changes in prevalence of parent–child co-residence in Japan." *Journal of Population Research* 10 (May): 25–36.

Hirschman, A. O. 1957. "Investment policies and dualism in underdeveloped countries." *American Economic Review.* (September): 533–565.

Hirschman, A. O. 1958. *The Strategy of Economic Development.* New Haven, CT: Yale University Press.

Hoselitz, Bert F. 1966. "Interaction between industrial and pre–industrial stratification systems." In *Social Structure and Mobility in Economic Development*, ed. Neil J. Smelser and Seymour Martin Lipset. Chicago: Aldine Publishing Company.

House, James S. 1980. *Occupational Stress and the Mental and Physical Health of Factory Workers.* Ann Arbor: Survey Research Center—Institute for Social Research, University of Michigan.

House, James S. 1981. *Work Stress and Social Support.* Reading, MA: Addison-Wesley.

House, James S. 1986. "Social support and the quantity and quality of life." Chap. 10, 253–269, in *Research on the Quality of Life*, ed. Frank M. Andrews. Ann Arbor: Survey Research Center—Institute for Social Research, University of Michigan.

House, James S. 1987. "Work and nonwork; support and conflict." In *Working–Life Research for the Future* (a volume in honor of Bertil Gardell), ed. Lennart Svensson and Heinz Leymann. Survey Research Center—Institute for Social Research, University of Michigan.

House, James S., A. J. McMichael, J. A. Wells, B. H. Kaplan, and L. R. Landerman. 1979. "Occupational stress and health among factory workers." *Journal of Health and Social Behavior* 20: 139–160.

Imanishi, Kinji. 1974. *Jinrui no Shinkashi* (History of Human Evolution). Tokyo: PHP Institute Press.

Inamura, Hiroshi. 1980. *Kateinai Boryoku: Nihongata Oyako Kankei no Byori* (Filial Violence: Pathology of the Parent–Child Relationship in Japan). Tokyo: Shinyo-sha.

Inkeles, Alex. 1973. "Making men modern: On the causes and consequences of individual change in six developing countries." Chap. 32, 342–361 in *Social Change: Sources, Patterns, and Consequences*, ed. Amitai Etzioni and Eva Etzioni-Halevy. 2nd ed. New York: Basic Books.

Inkeles, Alex, and David H. Smith. 1974. *Becoming Modern: Individual Change in Six Developing Countries.* Cambridge, MA: Harvard University Press.

Institute of Labor Administration. 1986. "Tenkin wo meguru kakushu toriatsukai no jittai" (Problems related to job transfer). September.

Institute of Population Problems, Ministry of Health and Welfare. 1989. *Jinko Tokei Shiryo Shu: 1988* (Latest Demographic Statistics of 1988). Research Series No. 260.

Institute of Population Problems, Ministry of Health and Welfare. 1990. *Jinko Tokei Shiryo Shu: 1989* (Latest Demographic Statistics of 1989). Research Series No. 264.

Institute of Population Problems, Ministry of Health and Welfare. 1992. *Jinko Tokei Shiryo Shu: 1992* (Latest Demographic Statistics of 1992). Research Series No. 273.

Institute of Population Problems, Ministry of Health and Welfare. 1993a. *Jinko*

Tokei Shiryo Shu: 1993 (Latest Demographic Statistics of 1993). Research Series No. 278.

Institute of Population Problems, Ministry of Health and Welfare. 1993b. "Nihon no setaisuno shorai suikei: Heisei 2-Heisei 22" (Statistical projections of the family and household in Japan: 1990–2020). November.

Institute of Population Problems, Ministry of Health and Welfare. 1993c. "The 10th demographic survey: Marriage and birth." September.

Institute of Population Problems, Ministry of Health and Welfare. 1994. "The 10th demographic survey: Marriage and birth, and special analyses on singles." May.

International Cultural Exchange Symposium, ed. 1989. *Between Understanding and Misunderstanding—problems of and prospects for U.S.-Japan cultural exchange.* Proceedings held at Aoyama Gakuin University Research Institute, Tokyo: Aoyama Gakuin University Research Institute. June 12–13.

International Labour Organization. 1989. *Yearbook of Labour Statistics: 1988.* Geneva: ILO.

Iriye, Akira. 1989. "The significance of cultural factors in contemporary international relations." Pp.62–63 in "Between understanding and misunderstanding—problems of and prospects for U.S.–Japan cultural exchange," ed. International Cultural Exchange Symposium, Tokyo: Aoyama Gakuin University Research Institute.

Irving, Bruce. 1988. "Mad about *manga*." *Northwest* (March): 30–31, 55–56, 61.

Ishida, Eiichiro. 1965. "Nihon bunka no patan" (The pattern of Japanese culture). *The Asahi*, December 1–12.

Ishihara, Shintaro. 1990. "Learning to say no to America." *Japan Echo* 17, (1): 29–35.

Ishihara, Shintaro, and Akio Morita. 1989. *"No" to Ieru Nihon* (A Japan That Can Say No). Tokyo: Kobunsha.

Ishikawa, K. 1986. "Ijime wa dare no sekinin ka" (Who is responsible for bullying?). *Voice* (March): 210–223.

Ishinomori, Shotaro. 1988. *Japan, Inc.: An Introduction to Japanese Economics (The Comic Book).* Berkeley: University of California Press.

Itagaki, Yoichi. 1960. "Some notes on the controversy concerning Boeke's 'dualistic theory': Implications for the theory of economic development in underdeveloped countries." *Hitotsubashi Journal of Economics* 1 (October): 13–28.

Ito, Masanori. 1985. *Sekai no Kyoiku Jijo: 18–ka–Koku no Kodomotachi* (Education around the World: Children in 18 Countries). Tokyo: Sanshusha.

Iwao, Sumiko, and Shigeru Hagiwara. 1987. *Ryugakusei ga mita Nihon—Junenme no Miryoku to Hihan* (Japan through Foreign Students' Eyes: Fantasies and Criticisms after Ten Years). Tokyo: Saimul-shuppan.

Iwata, Ryushi. 1977. *Nihonteki Keiei no Hensei Genri* (The Principle of Japanese Management). Tokyo: Bunshin–do.

Iwata, Ryushi. 1985. "Gakuseitachi ga mewo kagayasu toki—Musashi Daigaku deno jikken" (When students' eyes glitter: An experiment at Musashi University). Pp.166–181 in *Gendai no Espri*, ed. Shinbori Michiya. No. 213, Daigakusei—Dameron wo Koete (College Students: Beyond the Interpretation of Awful Students). Tokyo: Shibundo.

Jackson, James S., Linda M. Chatters, and Harold W. Neighbors. 1986. "The subjective life quality of black Americans." Chap. 7, 193–213, in *Research on the Quality of Life*, ed. Frank M. Andrews. Ann Arbor: Survey Research Center—Institute for Social Research, University of Michigan.

Japan Echo. 1989. "The Japanese Language." 16, Special Issue. *Japan Economic Journal*. 1987. "Shufu ni ryugaku netsu" (Fever of studying abroad among housewives). March 25.

Japan Economic Journal. 1989. "Nihonjin seito kyuzo—Genchiko ni omoi futtan" (Influx of Japanese students, heavy burden on local American schools). March 1.

Japan Economic Journal. 1990a. "R to L kikiwake 8–sai made ga shobu" (Age 8 would be the critical dividing point to distinguish sounds between r's and l's.) April 2.

Japan Economic Journal. 1990b. "Bei de gaikokugo kyoikunetsu" (An American fever for foreign language education). April 8.

Japan Economic Journal. 1990c. "Bei ni hojinmuke yochien" (A kindergarten for Japanese children in the United States). April 16.

Japan Economic Journal. 1990d. "Oshu de Nihongo kyoiku TV—BBC raishun kara" (BBC will broadcast programs on Japanese language education from spring of 1991). April 19.

Japan Economic Journal. 1990e. "Kyoiku no kokusaika, Nihon madamada: Beikokujin to ishiki de kakusa" (Internationalization of Japanese education has a long way to go: Attitudinal differences between the Japanese and Americans). May 15.

Japan Economic Journal. 1990f. "Kokoga fuben: Nichi-Bei seikatsu kozo kyogi" (U.S.-Japan life structural impediments initiative talks). June 24.

Japan Economic Journal. 1990g. " 'Kokoro no kagi' gakusei ga hiraku" (College students as big brothers and sisters: Assisting to alleviate school phobia). August 30.

Japan Economic Journal. 1992. "Koreika suru josei no shussan" (Japanese women giving birth later than ever before). August 10, evening edition.

Japan Economic Journal 1993a. "Kaigai chokusetsutoushi san–nen renzoku gensho" (The amount of Japan's foreign direct investments has been declining for over the past three years consecutively). May 9 morning edition.

Japan Economic Journal. 1993b. "Kekkon ni yori urumono" (What can be gained from marriage?). July 5 evening edition.

Japan Economic Journal. 1993c. "Josei no kanri noryoku yosei kenshu" (Seminar for training administrative skills among women). July 12 evening edition.

Japan Economic Journal. 1993d. "Manga necchuha benkyo mo dekiru" (Manga-addicts are also good students at school). July 13 morning edition.

Japan Economic Journal. 1993e. "Joshi gakusei no shushoku sensen" (Job seeking activities among women college students). July 15 evening edition.

Japan Economic Journal. 1993f. "Asobenai kodomotachi" (Children who cannot play). August 6 evening edition.

*Japan Economic Journal.*1993g. "Mentor jittai chosa" (Realities of the mentor system). August 21 evening edition.

Japan Economic Journal. 1993h "Sekuhara de komaranutameni" (How to prevent being victimized by sexual harassment) August 25.

Japan Economic Journal. 1993i. "Dai 9-kai wakamono chosa kekka" (Reports on the ninth survey on youth). September 9 morning edition.

Japan Economic Journal. 1993j. "Koseisho chiho rojin taisaku wo honkakuka" (Ministry of Health and Welfare strengthens programs for elderly suffering from senile dementia). November 28 morning edition.

Japan Economic Journal. 1994a. "Dai 46-kai shohisha chosa" (The forty-sixth survey on Japanese consumers). January.

Japan Economic Journal. 1994b "Fuman no juku ya kateikyoushi no keiyaku haki ga kanoni" (You can cancel contracts with unsatisfactory juku or tutors). February 1 morning edition.

Japan Economic Journal. 1994c. "Gaikokujin ryugakusei 5–mannin wo koeru" (Foreign students exceed 50,000). March 5 morning edition.

Japan Economic Journal. 1994d. "Kosei, Rodo wo togo 'kokuminseikatsu-sho' ni" (Merging the Ministry of Health and Welfare and the Ministry of Labor to make the 'Ministry of the People's Life'). March 26 morning edition.

Japan Economic Journal. 1994e. "Yobosesshuha? ryukobyoha?—kaigaino iryojijo wo shokai" (Immunization? Epidemic disease? Introducing medical affairs in foreign countries). April 3 morning edition.

Japan Economic Journal. 1994f. "Minkan sheruta, kakekomu tsuma atotatazu" (An increasing number of women seek private shelters). April 22 evening edition.

Japan Overseas Educational Services. 1993. *Kaigai Shijo Kyoiku* (Education for Japanese Children Abroad). September.

Japan Statistical Bureau of the Prime Minister's Office. 1991. *Japan Statistical Yearbook.* Vol. 39.

Japan Youth Research Institute. 1992. "Kokosei yujin-koibito chosa: Nichibei hikaku hokokusho" (Survey report on acquaintances and close friends of high school students in Japan and the U.S.A.). February.

Japan Youth Research Institute. 1993a. "Koko kyoiku nichibei hikaku hoko-kusho" (Survey report on high school education in Japan and the U.S.A.). March.

Japan Youth Research Institute. 1993b. "Chugakusei no seikatsu chosa: Nichi-bei hikaku hokokusho" (Survey report on the life of junior high school students in Japan and the U.S.A.). March.

Japan Youth Research Institute. 1994. "Kokosei life–style chosa: Nichi–Bei–Tai sankakoku hikaku" (Comparative studies of lifestyles of high school students in Japan, the U.S.A., and Taiwan). May.

Japanese Association of International Education. 1994. "93–nendo shihi gai-kokujin ryugakusei seikatsu jittai chosa" (Survey research on the life of foreign students studying in Japan with private funds). May.

Japanese Association of Sexual Education. 1992. "Seishonen to manga-kommikusu ni kansuru chosa" (Survey report on youth and manga/com-ics in Japan). June.

JETRO: Japan External Trade Organization. 1989. *Nippon 1989: Business Facts & Figures*. Tokyo: JETRO.

Johnson, Chalmers. 1982. *MITI and the Japanese Miracle*. Stanford, CA: Stan-ford University Press.

Johnson, Erwin H. 1964. "The stem family and its extensions in present-day Japan." *American Anthropologist* 66 (4): 839–851.

Johnson, Sheila K. 1988. *The Japanese through American Eyes*. Stanford: Stan-ford University Press.

Journal of Japanese Studies. 1989. 15 (1), Special Issue.

Kato, Hidetoshi, Tadao Umesao, Shuichi Kato, Shuntaro Ito, and Osamu Mi-zutani. 1989. "The globalization of Japanese: A roundtable." *Japan Echo* 16, (Special Issue): 61–68.

Kawabata, Yasunari. 1937. *Yukiguni* (The Snow Country). Tokyo: Sogensha.

Keizai Doyukai (Japanese Federation of Business Leaders). 1994. "Otoko to onna no ii kankei—tatemae to honne no aida de yureru chuken sarariman karano messeiji" (Amicable relationships between men and women: Messages from middle-level salaried-men in the midst of conflicts be-tween tatemae and honne). April.

Kelley, Allen C., Jeffrey G. Williamson, and Russell J. Cheetham. 1972. *Du-alistic Economic Development: Theory and History*. Chicago: University of Chicago Press.

Kessler, Ronald C. 1979. "Stress, social status, and psychological distress." *Journal of Health, Science and Behavior* 20: 259–272.

Kessler, Ronald C., and P. D. Cleary. 1980. "Social class and psychological distress." *American Sociological Review* 45:63–78.

Kessler, Ronald C., and M. Essex. 1982. "Marital status and depression: The importance of coping resources." *Social Forces* 61: 484–507.

Kessler, Ronald C., and J. A. McRae. 1981. "Trends in the relationship between sex and psychological distress: 1957–1976." *American Sociological Review* 46: 443–452.

Kitagawa, Joseph M. 1983. "Religion and modernization." *Kodansha Encyclopedia of Japan*. Vol. 6. Tokyo: Kodansha International.

Kobayashi, R. 1960. "Nihon keizai no niju kozo ni tsuite" (On the dual structure of the Japanese economy). *Keizai Seminar* 40. (February): 1–7.

Kumagai, Fumie. 1977. "The effects of cross-cultural education on attitudes and personality of Japanese students." *Sociology of Education* 50 (Jan.): 40–47.

Kumagai, Fumie. 1979a. "Social class, power and husband-wife violence in Japan." *Journal of Comparative Family Studies* 10 (1): 91–105.

Kumagai, Fumie. 1979b. "Family egalitarianism in cultural contexts: High-variation Japanese egalitarianism vs. low-variation American egalitarianism." *Journal of Comparative Family Studies* 10 (3) 315–329.

Kumagai, Fumie. 1979c. "America no kokosei, Nihon no kokosei—America kara no bunseki" (High school students in America and Japan). Chap. 9, 161–171, in *Nichibei Kokosei Hikaku Chosa* (Cross–cultural Studies of High School Students in America and Japan). Tokyo: Japan Youth Research Institute.

Kumagai, Fumie. 1981a. "Katei to Boryoku" (The Family and Violence). *Gendai no Espri* (L'esprit d'aujourd'hui). No. 166. Tokyo: Shibundo.

Kumagai, Fumie. 1981b. "Filial violence: A peculiar parent-child relationship in the Japanese family today." Pp. 337–349 in *Family and Household in Changing Japan* (Special Issue of the *Journal of Comparative Family Studies*, Vol. 12 [3]), ed. Takashi Koyama, Kiyomi Morioka, and Fumie Kumagai.

Kumagai, Fumie. 1982. "Metaphors and aging in the Japanese family." Paper presented at the University of British Columbia, Research Symposium on Aging, June 19–22.

Kumagai, Fumie. 1983a. "Filial violence in Japan." *Victimology* 8 (3): 173–194.

Kumagai, Fumie. 1983b. "Changing divorce in Japan." *Journal of Family History* 8 (1): 85–108.

Kumagai, Fumie. 1984a. "The life cycle of the Japanese family." *Journal of Marriage and the Family* 46: 191–204.

Kumagai, Fumie. 1984b. "Aging in the world and the elderly in Japan." Vol. 2, 211–243, in *Aging Well through Living Better*, ed. International Center of Social Gerontology. Paris, France: International Center of Social Gerontology.

Kumagai, Fumie.1985a. *Marginalization no Seishun* (A Process of Marginalization). Tokyo: YMCA Press.

Kumagai, Fumie. 1985b. "Japan's 'silver market' and aging society." *Journal of Japanese Trade and Industry* 4 (2): 45–48.

Kumagai, Fumie. 1986a. "Nihon no kazoku no nijyu kozo" (The dual structure of the Japanese family). *Shakaigaku Hyoron* (Japanese Sociological Review) 36 (4): 406–423.

Kumagai, Fumie. 1986b. "Modernization and the family in Japan." *Journal of Family History* 11 (4): 371–382.

Kumagai, Fumie. 1987a. "Satisfaction among rural and urban Japanese elderly in three-generation families." *Journal of Cross-Cultural Gerontology* 2 (3): 225–240.

Kumagai, Fumie, ed. 1987b. *Kaso to Kamitsu ni Ikiru Sansedai no Nihonjin* (Three Generations of the Japanese in the Underpopulated and Overpopulated Regions: For the Construction of an Integrated Social System). Tokyo: Toyota Foundation.

Kumagai, Fumie. 1988a. "Sama gawari no Nihonjin kazoku" (Changing situations of Japanese families in America). *Japan Economic Journal*, March 11.

Kumagai, Fumie. 1988b. "Nihonteki keiei no Beikoku iten—rinen ya bunka wa susumazu" (Japan's direct investment in the U.S.A.: Cultural frictions). *Japan Economic Journal*, October 12.

Kumagai, Fumie. 1988c. *Kokusaika Shakai no Katei Kyoiku* (Japanese Family Education in the Era of International Society). Tokyo: Kobundo-shuppansha.

Kumagai, Fumie. 1989a. "Psychological, cultural, and structural determinants of life quality of the Japanese family within the scope of Japan's direct investment in the U.S.A." Mimeographed.

Kumagai, Fumie. 1989b. "Beikoku funin de kazokuwa? (Are the Japanese families in America adjusted?) *Japan Economic Journal*. September 8.

Kumagai, Fumie. 1989c. "Taibei chokusetsutoshika ni okeru kodomo no tekio" (Adjustment of the Japanese children within the scope of Japan's direct investment in the U.S.A.) Paper presented at the Japan Educational Sociology annual meetings held in Tokyo, October.

Kumagai, Fumie. 1989d. "Taibei chokusetsutoshika ni okeru kazoku no tekio" (Adjustment of the Japanese family within the scope of Japan's direct investment in the U.S.A.) Paper presented at the Japanese Sociological Association annual meetings held in Tokyo, October.

Kumagai, Fumie. 1989e. "Japanese families abroad." *International Migration* 27 (4): 595–600.

Kumagai, Fumie. 1990a. "Taibei chokusetsutoshika ni okeru Nikkei kigyo no tekio—jugyoin to sono kazoku no jittai" (Adjustment of Japanese industries in the U.S.A. under the scope of direct investment: Local employees and Japanese families). Kagaku Gijutsu to Keizai no Kai, ed., *Kenkyu Kaihatsu Globalization*, pt. 2: 5–18.

Kumagai, Fumie. 1990b. "Bridging communication gaps between Japan and the United States." *Journal of Kyorin University* 2: 138–156.

Kumagai, Fumie. 1990c. "Cross–cultural perspectives on the Japanese family and policies." Chap. 10, 213–246, in *The Family as an Asset: An Inter-*

national Perspective on Marriage, Parenthood and Social Policy, ed. Stella R. Quah. Singapore: Times Academic Press.

Kumagai, Fumie. 1990d. "Changing fertility in Japan." *NWEC* (National Women's Education Center of Japan) Newsletter, vol.7, (2).

Kumagai, Fumie. 1991. "Amerika genchiseisan no hikakubunkaronteki kosatsu—Amerikajin jugyoin no nihonteki keiei ninshiki" (A comparative analysis of attitudes and perceptions of American workers toward Japanese-style management within the scope of Japan's direct investments in the United States). Chap. 10 in *Nihonteki Keiei-seisan Shisutemu to Amerika* (Japanese-style Management and Production System in the United States), ed. Tetsuo Abo. Kyoto: Minelva–shobo.

Kumagai, Fumie. 1992a. "An introductory chapter to *Japanese Families: A Century of Changes and Variations.*" *Kyorin University, Review of the Faculty of Foreign Languages*, 4: 93–117.

Kumagai, Fumie. 1992b. "Research on the family in Japan." Chap. 3, 159–237, in *The Changing Family in Asia: Bangladesh, India, Japan, Philippines, and Thailand*, ed. UNESCO. Bangkok: UNESCO Principal Regional Office for Asia and the Pacific.

Kumagai, Fumie. 1993a. "Nihonteki nijukozo bunka no kaigai itenn—Amerika genchiseisan no hikakubunkaronnteki kousatsu" (Transferring Japanese dual structural culture into the U.S.A.: Impact of Japan's direct investments on American workers). *Bulletin of the Culture Research Institute of Nihon University* 24: 29–74.

Kumagai, Fumie. 1993b. "Transferring Japanese dual structure into the American context: Success or failure? *Kyorin University, Review of the Faculty of Foreign Languages* 5: 12–47.

Kumagai, Fumie. 1993c. "Nihon no taibei chokusetsutoushi—keizaikoka, chiikiwa kokan" (Impact of Japan's direct investments in America: Favorable attitudes toward regional economies). *Japan Economic Journal*, November 27, morning edition.

Kumagai, Fumie. 1994a. "Nihonbunka no tokushitsu to kokusai kouryu" (Characteristics of Japanese culture and intercultural exchange). Chap. 5, 139–168 in *Nihon Bunkaron heno Sekkin* (Close–ups of Japanese Culture), ed. the Culture Research Institute of Nihon University. Tokyo: Sobunsha.

Kumagai, Fumie. 1994b. "Families in Asia: Beliefs and Realities." *Kyorin University, Review of the Faculty of Foreign Languages* 6: 99–113.

Kumagai, Fumie. 1994c. "America jugyoin no genchi Nihon kojo ninshiki—hikakubunkaronteki kosatsu" (Attitudes of American workers under the scope of Japan's direct investments in the U.S.A.). Chap. 9 in *Nihonteki Keiei Shisutemu to America* (Japanese Management in the American Context), ed. Tetsuo Abo. Kyoto: Mineruva-shobo.

Kumagai, Fumie. 1994d. "South rising again on foreign investments." *The Nikkei Weekly*, January 24.

Kurita, Wataru. 1990. "School phobia." *Japan Quarterly* 37 (3): 298–303.

Kurodo, Toshio. 1988. "A new perspective for the process of aging in Japan." A paper presented for the U.S.-Japan Seminar on Aging. Tokyo, September.

Kuroha, Ryoichi. 1988. "U.S. universities come to town." *Japan Quarterly* 35 (3): 271–274.

Lavee, Yoav, Hamilton I. McCubbin, and David H. Olson. 1987. "The effect of stressful life events and transitions on family functioning and well-being." *Journal of Marriage and the Family* 49 (4): 847–873.

Lazarus, R. S. 1981. "The stress and coping paradigm." Pp. 173–209 in *Theoretical Bases for Psychopathology*, ed. C. Eisdorfer, D. Cohen, A. Kleinman, and P. Maxim. New York: Spectrum.

Lebra, Takie S. 1984. *Japanese Women: Constraint and Fulfillment*. Honolulu: University of Hawaii Press.

Lee, Sang M., and Gary Schwendiman, eds. 1982. *Japanese Management: Cultural and Environmental Considerations*. New York: Praeger Publishers.

Leibenstein, Harvey. 1957. *Economic Backwardness and Economic Growth*. New York: Wiley.

Leibenstein, Harvey. 1960. "Technical progress, the production function and dualism." *Banca Nazionale del Lavoro Quarterly Review* (Dec.): 13–15.

Lestima, Robert, Robert L. August, Betty George, and Lois Peak. 1987. *Japanese Education Today: A Report from the U.S. Study of Education in Japan*. Washington, D.C.: U.S. Department of Education.

Levy, Ian Hideo. 1990. "The victory of the Japanese language: Exploding the myth of ethnic unity." *Japan Echo* 17 (1): 76–80.

Life and Cultural Bureau of the Metropolitan Tokyo Office. 1994. "Joseimondai ni kansuru kokusai hikaku chosa" (Cross–cultural comparative studies on the problems of women). April.

Life Insurance Cultural Center, ed. 1992. "Josei no seikatsu ishiki ni kansuru chosa" (Attitudes toward life among Japanese women). November.

Lin, Nan, and Walter M. Ensel. 1989. "Life stress and health: Stressors and resources." *American Sociological Review* 54: 382–399.

Litwak, Eugine. 1960a. "Occupational mobility and extended family cohesion." *American Sociological Review* 25: 9–21.

Litwak, Eugine. 1960b. "Geographic mobility and extended family cohesion." *American Sociological Review* 25: 385–394.

Lutz, Vera C. 1958. "The growth process in a 'dual' economic system." *Banca Nazionale del Lavoro Quarterly Review* (September) 9:13–15.

Maddox, George L., and D.C. Delinger. 1978. "Assessment of functional status in program evaluation and resources allocation model." *Annals of the American Academy of Political and Social Science* 438 (July): 59–70.

Management and Coordination Agency. 1990. "Chaju shakai ni okeru danjob-etsu no ishiki no keiko ni kansuru chosa kekka no gaiyo" (Attitudes of Japanese men and women toward aging society).

Management and Coordination Agency. 1994. "Nihon no suikei jinko" (Population estimates of Japan as of October 1, 1993). March.

Mancini, J. A. 1978. "Leisure satisfaction and psychological well-being in old age: Effects of health and income." *Journal of the American Geriatrics Society* 26: 550–552.

Matsubara, Haruo, and Fumie Kumagai, eds. 1982. "Konai Boryoku" (Violence in School). *Gendai no Espri*, No. 180. Tokyo: Shibundo.

Ministry of Agriculture. 1990. *Agriculture Census.*

Ministry of Construction. 1990. *White Paper on Construction: 1990.* July 17.

Ministry of Education. 1986. "Kikokushijo kyoiku no tebiki—sho-chu gakko hen no kanko ni tsuite" (Manual for education of returnee children: Elementary and junior high schools). *Monbu Jiho*, No.1315 (October): 72–75.

Ministry of Education. 1990. "Gakko kihon chosa sokuho: 1990" (The advance report on the basic survey of schools: As of May 1, 1990). August.

Ministry of Education. 1991. "Ryugakusei ukeire chosa" (A report on foreign students in Japan as of May 1990). February.

Ministry of Education. 1993a. "Gakko kihon chosa sokuho" (Advance report of the basic survey on schools: 1993). August.

Ministry of Education. 1993b. "91-nendo kyoikuhi chosa" (Survey on the cost for children's education: 1991). August.

Ministry of Education. 1993c. "Heisei 5-nendo shiritugakko itsuka–sei chosa" (Statistics on the 5–day a week school system among private schools). September.

Ministry of Education. 1993d. "Toko kyohi jido–seito ni kansuru kikitori chosa kekka" (Report on survey interviews on elementary and junior high school students suffering from school phobia). November.

Ministry of Education. 1993e. "Seito shidojo no shomondai no genjo to Monbusho no shisaku ni tsuite" (Problems relating to junior and senior high students and policies of the Ministry of Education). December.

Ministry of Education. 1994a. "92-nendo koko chutaisha chosa" (Studies on senior high school dropouts in 1992). February.

Ministry of Education. 1994b. "1993–nen zainichi ryugakusei chosa" (Survey on foreign students studying at higher educational institutions in Japan as of May 1993). February.

Ministry of Foreign Affairs. 1989. "Heisei Gan–nendo gakureiki zairyuhojin shijyo su chosa" (Report on Japanese school–age children abroad in 1989, as of May 1, 1989).

Ministry of Health and Welfare. 1990a. *Heisei gan–nendo–ban Kosei Hakusho* (The White Paper on Japanese Social Welfare: 1989).

Ministry of Health and Welfare. 1990b. "1989-nen jinkodoutai shakai keizaimen chosa—sonenki no kyubyoshi (tokushu)" (Socioeconomic studies on the Japanese population, special topic on sudden deaths among middle–aged working people).

Ministry of Health and Welfare. 1993a. "Seimei hyo" (Life expectancy table).

Ministry of Health and Welfare. 1993b. "Nihon no hyakusai ijo koreisha chosa" (Japanese very old elderly: survey of all the elderly 100 years old and over).

Ministry of Health and Welfare. 1994. "93 nendo kenko mappu" (The level of health by prefecture in 1993). May.

Ministry of Jurisdiction. 1994. "93-nen no shutsu–nyukoku–sha toukei" (Statistics of Japanese people going abroad and foreigners coming to Japan in 1993). May.

Ministry of Labor. 1990. *White Paper on Labor Economy in Japan: 1990*. July 27.

Ministry of Labor. 1993a. "Rifuresshu kyuka chosa" (Survey on the refresh–holiday program). August.

Ministry of Labor. 1993b. "Koreika shakai ni taioshita koreisha koyo taisaku ni kansuru toshin: Koyo shingikai" (Recommendations for the policy on the elderly workforce in the era of aging society by the Committee for the Labor Force Problems). December.

Ministry of Labor. 1994. "Sogo-shoku Josei no Shuugyo Jittai Chosa" (Survey on the realities and attitudes of Japanese women holding comprehensive career-track positions).

Mitsubishi Corp. ed. 1987. Tatemae *and* Honne—*Good Form and Real Intention in Japanese Business Culture: 500 Key Concepts Defined in Everyday English*. New York: Free Press.

Moeran, Brian. 1989. *Language and Popular Culture in Japan*. Manchester, United Kingdom: Manchester University Press.

Moore, Donald. 1988. *The Japanese Mind: Essentials of Japanese Philosophy and Culture*. Tokyo: C. Tuttle.

Morioka, Kiyomi. 1967. "Life cycle patterns in Japan, China, and the United States." *Journal of Marriage and the Family* 29 (3): 595–606.

Morioka, Kiyomi. 1981a. "Introduction: The development of family sociology in Japan." Pp. i–xiii in *Family and Household in Changing Japan*, (Special Issue of the *Journal of Comparative Family Studies*, vol. 12, ed. Takashi Koyama, Kiyomi Morioka, and Fumie Kumagai.

Morioka, Kiyomi. 1981b. "Family and housing over the life cycle." Pp. 365–396 in *Family and Household in Changing Japan* (Special Issue of the *Journal of Comparative Family Studies*, vol. 12 [3]), ed. Takashi Koyama, Kiyomi Morioka, and Fumie Kumagai.

Mouer, Ross, and Yoshio Sugimoto. 1986. *Images of Japanese Society: A Study in the Structure of Social Reality*. London: Kegan Paul.

Mouer, Ross, and Yoshio Sugimoto. 1988. *Constructs for Understanding Japan*. London: Kegan Paul.

Nakamura, Ryoei, and Kinosuke Odaka, eds. 1989. *Niju Kozo* (The Dual Structure). Tokyo: Iwanami Shoten.

Nakane, Chie. 1970. *Japanese Society*. Berkeley: University of California Press.

Nakano, Osamu. 1988. "A sociological analysis of the 'new breed.' " *Japan Echo* 15 (Special Issue): 12–16.

Nakatsu, Ryoko. 1989. "The trials of bilingual children." *Japan Echo* 16 (Special Issue): 58–60.

Nasu, Soichi. 1962. *Rojin Sedai Ron* (The Elderly Generations). Tokyo: Ashishobo.

National Land Agency. 1994. "Daitoshi-ken no jinko doko" (Demographic trends of greater city areas). May.

National Police Agency. 1994. "93-nen chuno jisatsu to iede" (Suicides and run-aways in 1993). April.

Nelson, Janet. 1984. "The effects of modernization upon the lives of Japanese women." Unpublished paper.

Neugarten, Bernice L. 1971. " 'Grow old along with me! The best is yet to be.' " *Psychology Today* 5(7): 45.

Neustupny, Jiri V. 1987. *Communicating with the Japanese*. Tokyo: Japan Times.

Nihon Mirai Gakkai, ed. 1989. *Nihongo wa Kokusaigo ni Naruka* (Can Japanese Be an International Language?). Tokyo: TBS Britannica.

Nihon University Population Research Institute. 1993. "Nihon no jinko suikei" (Projections for Japanese population).

Nikkei Ryutsu Shimbun. 1989. "Joshidaiseino ishiki to shohidoukou chosa" (Research on female college students attitudes and consumer behaviors). November.

Nimkoff, M. F. 1965. *Comparative Family Systems*. Boston: Houghton Mifflin.

Nippon Steel Human Resources Development Co., Ltd., ed. 1988. *Nippon: The Land and Its People*. 3rd ed. Tokyo: Gakusai-sha. 1988.

Nishimura, Hidetoshi. 1987. "Universities—under pressure to change." *Japan Quarterly* 34 (2): 179–184.

Oda, Susumu. 1990. "Religion in the age of parody." *Japan Echo* 17 (Special Issue): 68–71.

Office for Women, Prime Minister's Office. 1993a. "Chiho kokyo dantai ni okeru josei mondai ni kansuru gyosei no suishin ni tsuite" (Report on the enforcement status of policies for women's issues in the public organizations at the local level). September.

Office for Women, Prime Minister's Office. 1993b. "Josei no seisaku kettei sankaku jokyo shirabe: Seiji-gyosei-shiho" (Report on women taking part in the national public offices in the area of politics, administration, and judiciary). September.

Office for Women, Prime Minister's Office. 1993. "Kuni no shingikai nado ni okeru josei iin no sankaku jokyo shirabe" (Survey report on women members in the national committees for governmental affairs). November.

Office of Aging, Prime Minister's Office. 1991. "Rojin no seikatsu to ishiki ni kansuru kokusai hikaku chosa kekka no gaiyo'' (Comparative studies of lifestyles and attitudes of the elderly). September.

Office of Aging, Prime Minister's Office. 1993. ''Koreisha no chiikishakai heno sanka ni kansuru chosa'' (Survey research on community activities of the elderly). September.

Office of the Personnel. 1993. ''Heisei 4-nendo ni okeru ippanshoku komuin no ikuji kyugyo nado shutoku jokyo'' (Civil servants taking child–rearing leaves of absence in the fiscal year 1992). November.

Ogose, Sunao. 1988. ''The ossification of university faculties.'' *Japan Quarterly* 35(2): 157–162.

Ortiz, Vilma, and Carlos H. Arce. 1986. ''Subjective analysis of life quality.'' Chap. 6:171–191, in *Research on the Quality of Life*, ed. Frank M. Andrews. Ann Arbor: Survey Research Center—Institute for Social Research, University of Michigan.

Otsuka, Eiji. 1988. ''Comic–book formula for success.'' *Japan Quarterly* 35(3): 287–291.

Palmore, Erdman B., and Daisaku Maeda. 1985. *The Honorable Elders Revisited*. Durham, NC: Duke University Press.

Park, Robert E. 1928. ''Human migration and the marginal man.'' *American Journal of Sociology* 33 (6): 881–893.

Passin, Herbert. 1965. *Japanese Education*. New York: Columbia University Press.

Patrick, Hugh T., and Ryuichiro Tachi eds. 1986. *Japan and the United States Today*. New York: Center on Japanese Economy and Business.

Pearlin, L. I., and C. Schooler. 1978. ''The structure of coping.'' *Journal of Health and Social Behavior* 19: 2–21.

Peek, Charles W., Judith L. Fischer, and Jeannie S. Kidwell. 1985. ''Teenage violence toward parents: A neglected dimension of family violence.'' *Journal of Marriage and the Family* 47: 1051–1058.

Police Agency. 1990. *Jisatsu Hakusho* (White Paper on Suicide).

Police Agency. 1993. *Jisatsu Hakusho* (White Paper on Suicide).

Prime Minister's Office. *Official Bulletin*. 1886.

Prime Minister's Office. 1986. ''Kazoku katei ni kansuru yoron chosa'' (Public opinion survey on the family and household).

Prime Minister's Office. 1990a. ''Jyosei no shugyo ni kansuru yoron chosa'' (A public opinion survey on women's working).

Prime Minister's Office. 1990b. ''Koreika no raifusutairu ni kansuru yoron chosa'' (Public opinion survey on lifestyles of aging society). March 3.

Prime Minister's Office. 1990c. ''Shakai ishiki ni kansuru yoron chosa'' (Public opinion survey of attitudes regarding social issues). June 1.

Prime Minister's Office. 1990d. ''Kagakugijutsu to shakai ni kansuru yoron chosa'' (Public opinion survey on science, technology, and society). July 1.

Prime Minister's Office. 1990e. "Shakaishihon no seibi ni kansuru yoron chosa" (Public opinion survey on social resources). July 15.

Prime Minister's Office. 1990f. "Kokumin seikatsu ni kansuru yoron chosa" (Public opinion survey of attitudes regarding the national life). September 29.

Prime Minister's Office. 1990g. "Seishonen Hakusho" (White Paper on Japanese Youth). December.

Prime Minister's Office. 1991. "Jyosei ni kansuru yoron chosa" (Public opinion survey on females). January 12.

Prime Minister's Office. 1992a. "Danjo byodo ni kansuru yoron chosa" (Public opinion survey on the equality of men and women).

Prime Minister's Office. 1992b. "Fujin no seikatsu to ishiki ni kansuru kokusai hikaku chosa" (Cross-cultural comparative studies on lifestyles and attitudes of women).

Prime Minister's Office. 1993a. "Danjo byodo ni kansuru yoron chosa" (Public opinion survey on the equality of sexes). March.

Prime Minister's Office. 1993b. "Shakai hosho no shoraizo ni kansuru ishiki chosa: Shakai hosho seido shingikai" (Studies on public pensions by the Committee on the System of Public Pensions). April.

Prime Minister's Office. 1993c. "Kokumin seikatsu ni kansuru yoron chosa" (Public opinion survey on the life of the Japanese people). September.

Prime Minister's Office. 1993d. "Koteki nenkin seido ni kansuru yoron chosa" (Public opinion research on the public pension system). November.

Prime Minister's Office. 1993e. "Josei no Genjo to Shisaku" (White Paper on Japanese Women: Realities and Policy Recommendations). December.

Prime Minister's Office. 1993f. "Seishonen Hakusho" (White Paper on Japanese Youth).

Prime Minister's Office. 1994a. "Koreiki no seikatsu image ni kansuru yoron chosa" (Public opinion survey on images of lifestyles in the later years). January.

Prime Minister's Office. 1994b. "Dansei no life–style ni kansuru yoron chosa" (Public opinion survey on the lifestyle of Japanese men). February.

Prime Minister's Office. 1994c. "Dai 24–kai shakai ishiki ni kansuru yoron chosa" (The twenty-fourth public opinion survey on social attitudes of the Japanese people). March.

Rabier, J. R. 1974. *Satisfaction et insatisfaction quant aux conditions de view dans les pays membres de la communaute europeenne.* Brussels: Commission of the European Communities.

Rauch, Jonathan. 1990. "The trouble with Japan." *American Enterprise* (March-April): 78–82.

Reischauer, Edwin O. 1946. *Japan: Past and Present.* Cambridge, MA: Harvard University Press.

Reischauer, Edwin O. 1978. *The Japanese.* Cambridge, MA: Harvard University Press.

Reischauer, Edwin O. 1988. *The Japanese Today: Change and Continuity*. Cambridge, MA: Belknap Press of Harvard University Press.

Rex, John H. 1959. "The plural society in sociological theory." *British Journal of Sociology* 10 (June): 114–124.

Richardson, Bradley, ed. 1981. *Business and Society in Japan*. New York: Holt Reinhart.

Richie, Donald. 1981. *Some Aspects of Japanese Popular Culture*. Tokyo: Shubun International.

Robertson, Ian. 1989. *Society*. New York: Worth Publishers.

Rodgers, Roy H., and G. Witney. 1981. "The family cycle in twentieth century Canada." *Journal of Marriage and the Family* 43: 727–740.

Rosenmayr, L., and E. Kockeis. 1963. "Propositions for a sociological theory of aging and the family." *International Social Science Journal* 15: 410–426.

Sapir, Edward. 1929. "The status of linguistics as a science." *Language* 5: 207–214.

Sawachi, Hisae. 1989. "The political awakening of women." *Japan Quarterly* 36 (4): 381–385.

Schieffelin, B. B., and E. Ochs. eds. 1986. *Language Socialization across Culture*. New York: Cambridge University Press.

Sewell, William H., and Oluf M. Davidsen. 1961. *Scandinavian Students on an American Campus*. Minneapolis: University of Minnesota Press.

Shanas, Ethel. 1979. *National Survey of the Elderly, Report to Administration on Aging*. Washington, D.C.: Department of Health and Human Services.

Shanas, Ethel, P. Towsend, D. Wedderburn, H. Friis, P. Milhoj, and J. Stehouwer. 1968. *Old People in Three Industrial Societies*. London: Routledge and Kegan Paul.

Shigaku Kyoiku Kenkyujo (Private Education Research Institute). 1986. "Gendai kokosei ishiki repoto" (Attitudes of high school students today). October.

Shimizu, Hiroaki. 1992. *Koreika Shakai to Kazokukozo no Chiikisei* (Regional Variations of the Family Structure in Japanese Aging Society). Tokyo: Jicho-sha.

Shin, D. C., K. D. Kim, and H. K. Lee. 1982. "Perceptions of quality of life in an industrializing country: The case of the Republic of Korea." *Social Indicators Research* 10: 297–317.

Shinohara, Miyohei. 1959. "Nihon keizai no niju kozo" (The dual structure of Japanese economies). In *Sangyo Kozo* (Industrial Structures), ed. Miyohei Shinohara. Tokyo: Shunjyu-sha.

Shishido, Toshio. 1983. "Modernization through industrialization." Mimeographed.

Shishido, Toshio. 1987. "Koreika shakai no fukushi seisaku: Informal bunya no katsuyo" (Social policies in Japanese aging society: Active utilization of informal services). Chap. 7, 84–91, in *Kaso to Kamitsu ni Ikiru San-*

sedai no Nihonjin (Three Generations of the Japanese in the Underpopulated and Overpopulated Regions: For the Construction of an Integrated
Social System), ed. Fumie Kumagai. Tokyo: Toyota Foundation.

Shitamori, Masumi. 1989. "College life today: The economics of indulgence."
Japan Echo 16 (2): 35–38.

Silver, R. L., and C. B. Wortman. 1980. "Coping with undesirable life events."
Pp. 279–340 in *Human Helplessness*, ed. J. J. Garber and M. E. P. Se-
ligman. New York: Academic Press.

Simmel, Georg. 1908. *Soziologie*. Leipzig: Duncker & Humblot.

Siu, Paul C. P. 1952. "The sojourner." *American Journal of Sociology* 58: 34–
44.

Smelser, Neil J., and Seymour Martin Lipset, eds. 1966. *Social Structure and
Mobility in Economic Development*. Chicago: Aldine Publishing Company.

Smith, Robert J. 1981. "Japanese village women: Suye-mura 1935–36." *Journal of Japanese Studies* 7 (2): 259–269.

Smith, Robert J. 1983. *Japanese Society: Tradition, Self, and the Social Order*.
Cambridge: Cambridge University Press.

Sofue, Takao. 1971. *Kenminsei—Bunkajinruigakuteki Kosatsu* (Anthropological
Analyses of Japanese Personalities by Prefecture). Tokyo: Chuo Koron-
sha.

Soldo, Beth J., and Emily M. Agree. 1988. "America's elderly." *Population
Bulletin*. 43:3.

Statistical Bureau of the Ministry of Health and Welfare. 1989. "Showa 62 nen
Kokumin Seikatsu Kiso Chosa" (Basic Survey of Japanese Life in 1988).

Statistical Bureau of the Ministry of Health and Welfare. 1990a. "Showa 63-
nen-do jinko dotai shakai-Keizai-men chosa (shussei) no gaikyo" (Summary of demographic statistics of 1989: Fertility behavior and the family
planning). May 3.

Statistical Bureau of the Ministry of Health and Welfare. 1990b. "Heisei gan-
nen jinko dotai tokei" (Demographic Statistics of 1989). June 9.

Statistical Bureau of the Ministry of Health and Welfare. 1990c. "Heisei gan-
nen Kokumin Seikatsu Kiso Chosa" (Basic Survey of Japanese Life in
1989). August 10.

Statistical Bureau of the Ministry of Health and Welfare. 1991. "Heisei 2-nen
Kokumin Seikatsu Kiso Chosa" (Basic Survey of Japanese Life in 1990).

Statistical Bureau of the Ministry of Health and Welfare. 1992. "Heisei 3-nen
Kokumin Seikatsu Kiso Chosa" (Basic Survey of Japanese Life in 1991).

Statistical Bureau of the Ministry of Health and Welfare. 1993a. "Heisei 4-nen
Kokumin Seikatsu Kiso Chosa" (Basic Survey of Japanese Life in 1992).

Statistical Bureau of the Ministry of Health and Welfare. 1993b. "Heisei 5-nen
Kokumin Seikatsu Kiso Chosa" (Basic Survey of Japanese Life in 1993).

Statistical Bureau of the Ministry of Health and Welfare. 1994. "Heisei 5-nen
Kokumin Seikatsu Kiso Chosa (Basic Survey of Japanese Life in 1993).

Statistical Bureau of the Prime Minister's Office. 1920–1975. *The National Census*.

Statistical Bureau of the Prime Minister's Office. 1980–1988. *Labor Force Survey*.

Statistical Bureau of the Prime Minister's Office. 1993. "Tokei kara mita wagakuni no koreisha—Keiro no hi ni chinande, No. 117" (Statistical information of the Japanese elderlies: Information No. 17). September 14.

Statistics Bureau of the Management and Coordination Agency. 1985. "Jutaku Tokei Chosa: 1983" (Housing Survey of 1983). March 31.

Statistics Bureau of the Management and Coordination Agency. 1990. "Jutaku Tokei Chosa: 1988" (Housing Survey of 1988). March 31.

Statistics Bureau of the Management and Coordination Agency. 1991. "1990-nen kokusei chosa hokoku-sho gaiyo" ((Summary of the National Census in 1990).

Statistics Bureau of the Management and Coordination Agency. 1993. "Dai 43-kai Nihon Tokei Nenkan" (Japan Statistical Yearbook: 1994) December.

Statistics Bureau of the Management and Coordination Agency. 1994a. "Nihon no suikei jinko" (Estimates of the Japanese population as of October 1, 1993). March.

Statistics Bureau of the Management and Coordination Agency. 1994b. "1993-nen jumin kihon daicho jinko ido houkoku" (Demographic mobility of 1993 based on the basic directory of residency). April.

Statistics Bureau of the Management and Coordination Agency. 1994c. "Nihon no 15-sai miman no kodomo no kazu" (The number of Japanese children under fifteen as of May 4, 1994). May.

Stewart E. C. 1972. *American Cultural Patterns: A Cross Cultural Perspective*. New York: Intercultural Press.

Stonquist, Everett C. 1935. "The problem of the marginal man." *American Journal of Sociology*, 41 (1): 1–12.

Stonquist, Everett C. 1937 *The Marginal Man*. New York: Charles Scribner & Sons.

Straus, Murray A. 1969. "Phenomenal identity and conceptual equivalence of measurement in cross-national comparative research." *Journal of Marriage and the Family* 31: 233–241.

Streib, Gordon F. 1965. "International relations: Perspectives of the two generations on the older person." *Journal of Marriage and the Family* 27: 469–476.

Sugata, Masaaki. 1988. "Shinto resurgence." *Japan Quarterly* 35 (4): 365–370.

Sumner, William G. 1906. *Folkways*. New York: New American Library.

Sutton, Robert I., and Robert L. Kahn. 1986. "Prediction, understanding, and control as antidotes to organizational stress." Chap. 13, 337–361 in *Research on the Quality of Life*, ed. Frank M. Andrews. Ann Arbor: Survey Research Center—Institute for Social Research, University of Michigan.

Suzuki, Takao. 1990. *Nihongo to Gaikokugo* (The Japanese Language and Foreign Languages). Tokyo: Iwanami–shoten.

Suzuki, Takao. 1993. "The difficulty of understanding the mechanism of Japanese culture." *Kyorin University, Review of the Faculty of Foreign Languages*, 5: 1–11.

Tajiri, Shunichiro. 1991. "Karoshi nintei toso no nakade manabu" (Learning in the process of court procedures of the sudden death due to working too hard). *Nihon no Kagakusha* (Japanese Scientists) 26 (1): 6–18.

Takada, Masatoshi. 1989. "Woman and man in modern Japan." *Japan Echo* 16 (2): 39–44.

Takeuchi, Kiyoshi. 1980. "Nichi–Bei kokosei hikaku chosa kara" (Comparative studies on high school students in Japan and the United States). Pp. 1–23 in Community, No. 58: *Nihon no Kokosei-America no Kokosei* (Japanese High School Students and American High School Students).

Takeuchi, Yasuo. 1990. "Japan: A giant matures." *Japan Echo* 17 (Special Issue): 2–6.

Taylor, Jared. 1983. *Shadow of the Rising Sun: A Critical View of the Japanese Miracle*. New York: Morrow.

Thornton, Arland, Ming-Cheng Chang, and Te-Hsiung Sun. 1986. "The quality of life of Taiwanees." Chap. 12, 301–335 in *Research on the Quality of Life*, ed. Frank M. Andrews. Ann Arbor: Survey Research Center—Institute for Social Research, University of Michigan.

Toda, Teizo. 1926. *Kazoku no Kenkyu* (Studies on the Family). Tokyo: Kobundo.

Toennies, Ferdinand. 1957. *Community and Society—Gemeinschaft und Gessellschaft*. Translated and edited by C. P. Loomis, East Lansing: Michigan State University Press.

Tsurumi, Shunsuke. 1987. *A Cultural History of Postwar Japan, 1945–1980*. London: Rutledge and Kegan Paul.

Turner, Jonathan H., and Edna Bonacich. 1980. "Toward a composite theory of middleman minorities." *Ethnicity* 7 (2): 144–158.

Turner, Ralph H. 1960. "Sponsored and contest mobility and the school system." *American Sociological Review* 25 (Dec.): 6.

Uehata, Tetsunojo. 1993. "Karoshi mondai no igakuteki kosatsu" (Medical analyses of the sudden death caused by working too hard)." *Nihon no Kagakusha* (Japanese Scientists) 28 (4): 324–336.

United Nations. 1956. *The Aging of Populations and Its Economic and Social Implications, Population Studies, No. 26*. New York: United Nations Printing Office.

United Nations. 1992. *U.N. Demographic Yearbook of 1990*. New York: United Nations.

United Nations. 1993. *Demographic Yearbook: 1993*. New York: United Nations Printing Office.

U.S. Department of Commerce. 1994. "World demographic outlook of 1994."

U.S. Department of Education. 1987. "Japanese education today: A report from the U.S. Study of Education in Japan."

U.S. Department of Health and Human Services. 1994. "Monthly report on the vital statistics." April.

Useem, Ruth H. 1973. "Third culture factors in educational change." Chap. 8 in *Cultural Challenges to Education: The Influence of Cultural Factors in School Learning*, ed. Cole S. Brembeck and Walker H. Hill. Lexington, MA: Lexington Books.

U.S. News & World Report. 1987. "Who's at the head of the class." January 19, 61.

U.S. News & World Report. 1990a. "The trade war gets personal." April 16, 38–40.

U.S. News & World Report. 1990b. "The coming global boom." July 16, 22–28.

van Wolferen, Karel G. 1989. *The Enigma of Japanese Power: People and Politics in a Stateless Nation*. London: Macmillan.

Varley, H. Paul. 1984. *Japanese Culture*. 3rd. ed. Honolulu: University of Hawaii Press.

Vogel, Ezra F. 1980. *Japan as No.1*. Cambridge, MA: Harvard University Press.

Wagatsuma, Hiroshi. 1984. "Some cultural assumptions among the Japanese." *Japan Quarterly* 31 (4): 371–379.

Wakita, Haruko. 1984. "Marriage and property in premodern Japan." *Journal of Japanese Studies* 10 (1): 88–98.

Wall Street Journal. 1982. "Families: Paying the price of social security." April 2, 22.

Warren, Carol. 1978. "Parent batterers: Adolescent violence and the family." Paper presented at the annual meetings of the Pacific Sociological Association, Anaheim, CA

Weingarten, Helen, and Fred B. Bryant. 1987. "Marital status and the meaning of subjective well-being: A structural analysis." *Journal of Marriage and the Family* 49, (4): 883–892.

White, Merry. 1987. *The Japanese Educational Challenge: A Commitment to Children*. New York: Free Press.

White, Theodor. 1985. "The danger from Japan." *New York Times*. November 16, A19.

Wilson, Dick. 1986. *The Sun at Noon: An Anatomy of Modern Japan*. New York: Hamish Hamilton.

Women's Bureau of the Ministry of Labor. 1990. "Fujin rodo no jitsujo" (White Paper on the Status of Japanese Women).

Women's Bureau of the Ministry of Labor. 1993. "Fujin rodo no jitsujo" (White Paper on the Status of Japanese Women).

Women's Bureau of the Ministry of Labor. 1993a. "Fujin rodo no jitsujo" (White Paper on the Status of Japanese Women).

Women's Bureau of the Ministry of Labor. 1993b. "Fujin rodo no jitsujo" (White Paper on the Status of Japanese Women). October.

Women's Bureau of the Ministry of Labor. 1993d. "Joshi shinki gakusotsu saiyo naitei nado chosa kekka" (Survey research report on employment situations of women who graduated from higher educational institutions in March 1993). December.

Women's Bureau of the Ministry of Labor. 1994. "Sogo-shoku josei no shugyo jittai chosa" (Survey research report on the realities of women holding comprehensive jobs at large–scale organizations). March.

Women's Educational Association, ed. 1989. *Tokei ni Miru Jyosei no Genjo: 1989*. (Statistical Presentations of the Status of Women in 1989). Tokyo: Kakiuchi Shuppan.

World Health Organization. 1988. *World Health Statistics Annual*. Geneva, Switzerland: WHO.

World Plaza. 1991. *Ryugakusei Tokushu* (Special Issue on Foreign Students in Japan), No.14 (February-March).

Yamashiro, Masaki. 1987. "The big welcome for foreign college students." *Japan Quarterly* 34 (1): 39–45.

Yano–Kota Memorial Society, ed. 1986. *Sujidemiru Nihon no Hyakunen* (A Century of Japanese History in Statistics). Tokyo: Kokusei–sha.

Yano–Kota Memorial Society, ed. 1989. *Nippon: A Charted Survey of Japan —1989/90*. Tokyo: Kokusei-sha.

Yano–Kota Memorial Society, ed. 1993. *Nihon Kokusei Zue: 1990* (A Charted Survey of Japan: 1990). Tokyo: Kokusei-sha.

Yasuba, Yasukichi. 1985. "Niju kozo ron" (On the dual structure). In *Keizai Hatten Ron* (Theories of Economic Development), ed. Yasukichi Yasuba and M. Ezaki. Tokyo: Sobun-sha.

Yoneyama, Toshio. 1976. *Nihonjin no Nakama Ishiki* (Group Identity of the Japanese). Tokyo: Kodan–sha.

Youth Bureau of the Management and Coordination Agency. 1990. *White Paper on Youth: 1990*. January.

Youth Bureau of the Management and Coordination Agency. 1993a. *1992-Nenban Seishonen Hakusho* (White Paper on Youth: 1993). January.

Youth Bureau of the Management and Coordination Agency. 1993b. "Seishonen to poruno kommiku ni kansuru jittai chosa" (Survey research on the Japanese youth and pornographic manga and comics). June.

Youth Bureau of the Management and Coordination Agency. 1994a. *1993-Nenban Seishonen Hakusho* (White Paper on Youth: 1994). January.

Youth Bureau of the Management and Coordination Agency. 1994b. "Sekai seinen ishiki chosa" (Comparative studies on the attitudes of youth). January.

Index

Africa, 48
"Age-cracy," 10, 21
Aging: baby boomer generations, 127;
  contributing factors, 124, 127–28, 136–
  37; declining birth rates, 127, 136, 136
  n.6; demographics, 124–26, 130, 136;
  increased life expectancy, 127–30; as a
  sociocultural process, 123–24. *See also*
  Elderly
Aichi, 132
Aid for Families with Dependent Elderly
  (AFDE), 153
Akita, 132
Allied occupation, 3–4, 62, 93–95, 100
Amae, 10
Americanization, 1, 3–4, 93–95, 100
Arranged marriage, 22, 28 n.21
Asia, 1–2, 47, 70; Japanese Saturday
  schools in, 48
Asia in comparison with Japan: attitudes
  of youth, 76, 89 n.9; elderly, 132, 137
  n.21, 151; female labor participation
  rates, 111–12; lifestyles of high school
  students, 80–81. *See also names of
  specific countries*

Asshi-kun, 31, 32
Australia, 33
Austria, 134

Baby boomer generations, 127, 145
Bali, Indonesia, 33
Battered wives, 104
Birth rates, 126, 136, 136 n.6
Buddhism, 2, 8–9
Bullying, 86–87

Canada, 24, 48, 142
Career-track positions, for women, 115–
  16, 118 n.27
Census Bureau of Japan, 17
Chiba, 18, 132, 135
Childbirth, 21, 102–3
China, 70, 112; thoughts and practices in
  Japan, 2
Chin-zoku, 33
Chonmage, 3
Christianity, 8–9
Christmas cake, women as, 31
Chu, 2, 9, 16
Chugoku, 4

Civil Code of 1898, 16, 94
Civil Code of 1947, 16, 62, 95
Class identification, 33–34
College students, 82–83, 90 n.26
Comic book culture, 74–75, 89 nn.5, 7
Confucianism, 2, 9, 16, 94–95, 123
Constitution of 1947, 95
Contest mobility, 65
Cost of living, 37
Council on Aging Society, 142
Cram school, 66–67
Cultural self-colonization, 2, 4

Dankai no sedai, 74
Democratization, 1, 3–4, 93, 95, 100
Divorce, 23–24, 27, 103
Doi, Takako, 96–97
Dosho imu, 104
Dual Structure, 4–5, 8, 22, 27, 54, 65–66, 157

Economic Planning Agency, 35–36, 38–39
Edo period, 9, 15–16, 94–95
Education: abroad, 47–50, 52–53, 55–57, 57 n.12, 68–69; bullying, 86–87; cost, 67, 83, 90 n.28; cram school, 66–67; cross-cultural impact, 68, 70–71; development, 61–62; dual structure, 65–66; examinations and, 64–66, 76, 78–80; family and, 67–68, 72 n.1; foreign students in Japan, 70–71; modern system, 62–67, 72 n.3; mother's role, 52, 66–67; Saturday school, 64–65; school phobia, 87–88; school violence, 83–85; standardization, 62. *See also* Youth
Elderly: attitudes toward, 123; families living abroad and, 53–54; health, 131–32; income, 140–41; labor force participation, 139–40, 142–43; living arrangements, 141, 147–54, 154 n.2, 155 n.8; marital status, 129, 131; primary care providers, 132–33, 135, 153–54; problems of, 124, 129, 131–33, 137, 152–54; regional variations, 132, 134–35, 149; retirement, 141–42; senile dementia, 135–36; silver market, 143–45, 146 n.13; social participation,

154, 155 n.17; suicide and, 134; very old elderly, 131–132, 137 nn.17, 18. *See also* Aging
Employment: ethics, 10; hours, 10, 12 n.12, 39. *See also* Elderly; Lifestyle; Modernization; Women, labor force participation
Engel's coefficient, 37
English as a Second Language (ESL), 50, 52–53
Equal employment opportunity, 112, 114–17
Equal Opportunity Law (EOL), 114–16
Eta, 15
Europe, 33, 48, 70
Europeanization, 1–3
Examination hell, 64–66, 76, 78–80

Family: changes in, 95; fertility behavior, 20–21; filial violence, 24, 85–86, 90 nn.30, 32; generational family, 19, 27; internalcharacteristics, 24–25; life cycle, 24; modified stem family, 25–27; nuclear family, 17–19, 25, 27; numbers of, 20; problemsof, social policies for, 47–56; regional variations, 27; relations in, 24–25, 33, 51; residence abroad, 47, 49–56; size, 20; stem family, 3, 11, 15–20, 22, 24–25, 94. *See also* Education; Elderly; Lifestyle; Marriage; Women
Fertility behavior, 20–21
Filial violence, 24, 85–86, 90 nn.30, 32
Foreign direct investment, 47–48
Foreign students in Japan, 70–71
France, 2, 36, 111, 140, 142

Gaijin, 158
Generational family, 19, 27, 150, 152
Genji Monogatari (Shikibu), 94
Geographical insularity, 1–2
Germany, 2–3, 36, 76, 132, 140, 142, 147
Giri, 10
Golden Plan, 153
Graying of Japan. *See* Aging; Elderly
Groupism, 9–10, 34
Gyaku tama, 32

Hata, Tsutomu, 97, 99
Heian period, 94
Hierarchical-vertical relationships, 4, 9–11, 16, 24–25
High school students, 64, 76–82
Hokkaido, 4
Homogeneity, 2, 9–10
Honmei-kun, 32
Honne, 10
Horizontal-egalitarian relationships, 4, 16, 25
Hosokawa, Morihiro, 97, 99; cabinet of, 97
House of Councilors, 96, 98–99, 105 n.8
House of Representatives, 97–99, 105 n.8
Housing, 38
Hungary, 134

Ie. See Family, stem family
Ijime, 86–87
Industrialization, 27
Internationalization, 42, 47, 54–55, 67, 157–59; cultural factors and, 158–59
Ippan-shoku, 114
Ishin denshin, 10
Ishinomori, Shotaro, 89 n.5
Italy, 142

Japan Economic Journal, 104
Japan Gynecological Association, 102
Japan Socialist Party (JSP), 96–97, 99
Japan Youth Research Institute, 76, 80
Japanese language, 10–11, 12 n.15
Japanese Saturday schools. *See* Education, abroad; Asia, Japanese Saturday schools in; United States, Japanese Saturday schools in
Juku, 66–67
Junior high school students, 75–77

Kagoshima, 132, 135
Kamakura period, 4
Kanagawa, 18, 135
Karoshi, 39–40
Kaso, 4–5
Kazoku, 33
Keep-kun, 31–32
Keizai Doyukai, 116

Kikokushijo, 67–68
Kimono, 3
Ko, 2, 9, 16
Kochi, 132, 135
Komori-zoku, 33
Korea, 70, 76, 111–12, 132, 140, 151
Korei shosanfu, 102
Kubiki, 134
Kumamoto, 132
Kyoiku-mama, 66
Kyushu, 4

Latin America, 70
Leisure Development Center, 41
Leisure-land syndrome, 83
Liberal Democratic Party (LDP), 96–97, 99
Life cycle, 24
Life expectancy, 127–30
Life GNP index, 41
Lifestyle: attitudes toward, 34, 36, 40–43, 44 nn.6, 10, 45 n.25; class identification, 33–34; cost of living, 37; housing, 38; impediments of, 42; quality of, 34, 36–43, 43 n.4, 44 n.15. *See also* Elderly; Family; Women; Youth
Lokku-zoku, 33
Longevity revolution, 127
Love marriage, 22, 28 n.21

Madonna power, 96–97
Makura no Soshi (Nagon), 94
Management and Coordination Agency, 39, 134
Manga, 116. *See also* Youth, comic book culture
Marriage, 21–22, 31–33; age and, 21–22, 31, 102, 105 n.19; arranged marriage, 22, 28 n.21; battered wives, 104; childbirth and, 102; cost, 32–33; divorce, 23–24, 103; husband-wife relationship, 103–4; love marriage, 22, 28 n.21. *See also* Elderly; Family; Women
Maternity Leave Law, 117
Matriarchal authority, 93–94
Matrilineal authority, 93–94
Meiji period, 64, 95
Meiji Restoration, 2, 9, 16, 62, 94

Middle East, 48
Ministry of Construction, 40
Ministry of Education, 55–56, 62, 64–65, 67, 70, 78, 83, 88
Ministry of Foreign Affairs, 48
Ministry of Health and Welfare, 55, 88, 131, 136
Ministry of Labor, 39, 55, 79, 114–15, 117 n.3, 141–42
Ministry of People's Life, 55
Ministry of Post and Telecommunications, 141
Mitsugu-kun, 31
Miyazawa, Kiichi, 97
Modernization, 1–2; allied occupation, 3–4, 93, 95, 100; culture, 1–4, 69; demographics, 5, 11 n.4; geographical insularity, 1–2; homogeneity, 9; human relations, 9–10; language, 10–11, 12 n.15; regional variations, 4–5, 11 nn.4, 5; results of, 4; status of women, 93, 95; working population, 5–8, 107. *See also* Family; Religion; Women
Modified stem family, 25–27
M-shaped curve, 111
Murayama, Tomiichi, 97, 99

Nagoya, 39
Nara period, 94
National Standard Index (NSI), 34, 36, 44 n.5
Nemawashi, 11
Nihongami, 3
Niigata, 134
North America, 47–48, 70
Nuclear family, 17, 19, 25–27, 148
Nuclearization of households, 17–19, 24–25, 27
Nure ochiba, 131

Obatarian, 96
Obon, 9
Okinawa, 132
On, 10
Orientalization, 1–2
Osaka, 132
Oyabun-kobun, 9

Patriarchal authority, 93–94
Peter Pan syndrome, 74
Police Agency, 85, 90 n.32
Politics, women in, 96, 98–100
Post-World War II, 16, 20, 25, 32, 62, 95. *See also* Modernization, allied occupation
Primary care providers, 132–33, 135, 153–55
Primary industry, 5–6, 107–8, 117 n.3
Prime Minister's Office, 33, 40, 76, 103

Quality oflife, 34, 36–43, 43 n.4, 44 n.15

Religion, 2, 8. *See also under specific names*
Retirement, 141–42
Ronin, 79–80
Rozu famili-zoku, 33
Rural areas: aging in, 133; divorce, 27; equal employment opportunity, 115; farming, 8; lifestyle, 5; living arrangements, 18–19, 149; marriage, 27; population, 4–5, 7–8
Russia, 76
Ryugaku. See Education, abroad

Saitama, 18, 132, 135
Samurai, 15, 61
San shuno jinki, 38, 44 n.16
Sanko, 32
Sanwa Bank, 32
Saturday school, 64–65
School phobia, 87–88
School violence, 83–85
Secondary industry, 6, 107–8, 117 n.3, 145
Seiko-totei, 132
Sempai-kohai, 9
Senile dementia, 135–36
Seniority-based system, 123
Sex roles, 100–103, 105 nn.11, 12
Shimane, 132, 135
Shinjinrui, 73–74, 89 n.5
Shinto, 2, 8
Shogunate, 15
Shukan Shonen Jampu, 75
Silver market, 142–45, 146 n.13

Sodaigomi, 131
Sogo-shoku, 114–15
South America, 48
Sponsored mobility, 65
Standardized education, 62
Stem family, 3, 11, 15–20, 22, 24–25, 94
Structural Impediments Initiative, 42
Suicide, 134
Sweden, 36, 76

Taiwan, 70, 80, 87
Tama no koshi, 32
Tanshin funin, 52, 67–68
Tatemae, 10
Terakoya, 61
Tertiary industry, 5–6, 107–8, 117 n.3,
   145
Thailand, 76
Third Culture Kids (TCKs), 67–68
Three Sacred Treasures, 38, 44 n.16
Three-generation family, 19, 27
Tohoku, 4
Toitsu chiho senkyo, 98
Tokyo, 18–19, 32, 37, 44 n.14, 70, 83,
   90 n.28, 135, 149
Toyama, 19
Tsukushinbo, 31, 32

United Kingdom, 2, 36, 41, 65, 132, 140,
   142, 147
United States: American attitudes toward
   Japanese, 54–55, 56 n.4; Japanese
   overseas assignments in, 50–53; Japanese Saturday schools in, 48–49
United States: in comparison with Japan:
   cost of living, 44 n.14; divorce, 23; education, 64–65, 82; elderly, 132, 137
   nn. 2, 3, 139–40, 142, 144, 150–53,
   154 n.1; income, 41; lifestyles of students, 80–82; living standards, 36, 41;
   marriage, 28 n.20; women, 24, 116;
   working hours, 10; youth, 76–77, 81–
   82
Urban areas: aging in, 135; divorce, 27;
   equal employment opportunity, 114;
   lifestyle, 5; living arrangements, 18–19,
   149; marriage, 27
Urbanization, 4, 27

Voting rates, 97–98, 105n.8

Wafuku, 3
Wakon kansai, 2
Wakon yosai, 2
Wayo secchu, 3
Western societies: in comparison with Japan: attitudes of youth, 76, 89 n.9; cost
   of living, 37; divorce, 23; education,
   65, 70, 82; elderly, 25, 124–25, 132,
   136 nn.2, 3, 137 n.21, 139–40, 142,
   147, 150–51; family relations, 25; female labor force participation, 111–13;
   life expectancy, 127; lifestyles, 41; living standards, 36, 40; marriage, 21–22,
   28 n.18; women, 24, 93; working
   hours, 10. *See also names of specific
   countries*
Westernization, 1–3
Women: attitudes toward sex roles, 100–
   103, 105 nn. 11, 12; childbirth, 21,
   102–3; divorce, 23, 27; education, 105
   n.19, 109; elderly and, 135; leadership
   and, 44; lifecycle pattern, 24; marriage,
   21–22, 27–28; peasant classes, 95; premodern era, 93–94; politics and, 96,
   98–100; post-war era, 95–96;
   relationships with men, 31–32; voting
   rates, 97–98, 105 n.8. *See also* Education; Elderly; Family; Lifestyle; Marriage; Modernization
Women: labor force participation: attitudes toward marriage and, 100–102,
   112; career-track positions, 115–16,
   118 n.27; education, 109, 114–15;
   equal employment, 112, 114–17; length
   of, 112; management positions, 112–
   13, 116; part-time work, 113; rates of,
   107–11, 117 n.3, 118 n.10; social support structures, 117

Yamagata, 19
Yofuku, 3
Yoma, 3
Youth, 73, 89 n.1; attitudes of, 74, 76,
   78, 90 n.19; college students, 82–83,
   90 n.26; comic book culture, 74–75, 89
   nn.5, 7; high school students, 64, 76–

82; junior high school students, 75–77; numbers of, 73, 89; problems of, 83–90; *shinjinrui*, 73–74, 89 n.5. *See also* Education; Family

Youth Development Headquarters, 90 n.32
Yutori, 34, 41

Za, 94
Zangyo, 39

About the Authors

FUMIE KUMAGAI is a Japanese sociologist holding an American doctorate with extensive experience in the West. She is currently a Professor of Sociology at the Graduate School of International Cooperations and Department of Foreign Studies at Kyorin University in Tokyo.

DONNA J. KEYSER is Associate Director of the Center on Japanese Economy and Business at Columbia University. Specializing in Japanese politics and international political economy, Keyser spent four years in Japan as a student, teacher, and Fulbright research fellow.